AF604655

Imprint

The original German was publishing by the German and Austrian Bishop conference.
Published in Australia by Freedom Publishing Books, 33 Scoresby Road, Bayswater, VIC Australia
Translated by Coventry Press.

Nihil Obstat: Reverend Monsignor Gerard Diamond MA (Oxon), LSS, D.Theol
Diocesan Censor

Imprimatur: Very Reverend Joseph Caddy AM Lic.Soc.Sci VG
Vicar General
Archdiocese of Melbourne

Date: 21 April 2020

Project Manager and Editor: Bernhard Meuser
Editorial Assistance: Claudia Weiß
Project Assistant: Clara Steber

Cover, Layout, Design, Illustrations by Alexander von Lengerke, Cologne, Germany

ISBN: 9780648725145
Cataloguing-in-Publication entry is available
from the National Library of Australia
http:/catalogue.nla.gov.au/
Printed in Australia by Brougham Press, 33 Scoresby Road, Bayswater, VIC 3153

www.youcat.org
From the proceeds of its publications and from donations, the not-for-profit YOUCAT
Foundation gGmbH supports worldwide projects of New Evangelization which
encourage young people to discover the Christian Faith as a foundation for their lives.
You can help further the work of the YOUCAT Foundation with your donations,
which can be made through:

Tweeting with GOD (#TwGOD) is a global multimedia initiative that can very well be used together with YOUCAT. #TwGOD consists of a book, an app for Android and iOS, manuals for youth leaders and a presence in social media.

More information from www.tweetingwithgod.com

10 9 8 7 6 5 4 3 2 1

YOUCAT

Understanding what it means to be a Christian

An introduction
in 26 units

FREEDOM PUBLISHING BOOKS MELBOURNE

Contents

Symbols and their meanings

Questions from YOUCAT

Quote from a Saint or celebrity

Quotations from Scripture

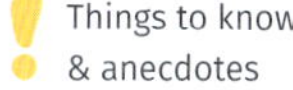
Things to know & anecdotes

Questions from "Tweeting with God"

MADRID 2011

Understanding the faith now!

In Chinese, they say, there is only one character for both "crisis" and "opportunity". Some people say that the Catholic Church is going through its greatest crisis in 500 years. So what would prevent us from saying that the Catholic Church has its greatest opportunity to renew itself?

What was the situation like for the early Christians? In the Epistle to Diognetus from the 2nd century we read: "They dwell in their own countries, but simply as sojourners. As citizens, they share in all things with others, and yet endure all things as if foreigners. Every foreign land is to them as their native country, and every land of their birth as a land of strangers. They marry, as do all others; they beget children; but they do not destroy their offspring. They have a common table, but not a common bed... They obey the prescribed laws, and at the same time surpass the laws by their lives.

... They are unknown and condemned; they are put to death, and restored to life... what the soul is in the body, that are Christians in the world."

Faced with the drive of the early Christians, the corrupt ancient Greek and Roman societies collapsed. Within a handful of generations, the disciples of Jesus had turned the known world upside down. So we can't help but wonder: how can we Catholic Christians regain the charisma we once had? What is our "great opportunity"? Let us take the early Christians as our measuring stick! What did they have that we don't? First of all they had a profile. Secondly, they had passion. And thirdly, they had courage.

How do we raise our profile? By having the courage to be different. Some now say that the Church must become more "normal", remain silent about miracles, conceal whatever stands out, smooth the edges, lower its standards and adapt to the world. Absurd! What consultant would advise Mercedes to build more normal cars, ignore its technical supremacy and take the humble Toyota Corolla as its role model!

The first Christians had the courage to be *challengingly different*. They were passionate about getting to know their faith. This distanced them somewhat from their contemporaries. People whispered about them, said bad things about them, even persecuted them only to convert to the "New Way" eventually. But what convinced them was the steadfast identity of the first Christians. They did not see their faith as just a nice idea that could be replaced by a more appropriate one at their convenience. They saw it as true and if necessary would let themselves be fed to the lions to prove it.

The book which offers the "profile" of the Catholic Church is the Catechism – The large CCC, but also YOUCAT which is the Catechism translated into a more understandable format. Since the Catechism makes no false compromises and clearly states the Church's common faith, some strategists for Church renewal are not in favour of it. Bishop Stefan Oster drew their ire when he announced that as bishop he wanted to fight for the integrity of the Faith. For example, he considers the contents of the Catechism to be true, "... essentially all of it – namely out of theological and philosophical conviction."

Many Catholics feel that now is the time to gain a clear identity and profile as a Catholic Christian!

- The "Course on Faith - Understanding what it means to be a Christian" is for all who yearn for the beauty and radiance of the Gospel.
- The author has tried to present the central points of the Gospel in as gripping a manner as a good film might recount them.
- Next to these accounts you can find YOUCAT questions (indicated by a Y) – as steps to lead you deeper into the Faith. You can follow them or just read the book.
- This Faith Course can be done alone. But it would be better to get together with friends, neighbours, people from the parish. The best way to gain conviction is through dialogue in a study group.
- To learn more about organising a study group and getting a free copy of the YOUCAT Study Guide for your smart phone, see page 170 of this book.

PS: Of course, there is much more to ask than can be found in the Catechism. YOUCAT is well complemented by the practical questions young people have put to Fr Michel Remery in "Tweeting with God". You can find some of these questions in this book. They are marked with a . For more on this fantastic initiative see page 180.

What do we know about God?

This is about

how people could
come up with the crazy idea
that apart from stones, animals, plants and themselves,
there could be something
extraterrestrial
that we should communicate with.

Question 41: Does science make the Creator superfluous?

Thus, for example, the question asked by philosopher **FWJ Schelling** (1775-1854): "Why is there something rather than nothing?"

Question 23: Is there a contradiction between faith and science?

Question 355: "You shall not have strange gods before me." What does that mean?

People have always been "religious". In fact, there probably isn't a single people or culture that has not worshipped something divine, or one or even multiple gods. "Why is there something rather than nothing?" is still the first question for philosophy even today. The answers given to it are similar; most people say: reality cannot be conceived of without God. The findings of modern natural science (e.g. about the Big Bang, chance and necessity, the origin and development of human life) do not fundamentally change this either.

Even the earliest testimonies of religion are filled with tokens of reverence, beauty, gratitude. People have spread flowers before the creator and sustainer of the world, let fragrant incense rise up to him and built magnificent temples to the *mysterious creator of all things*. At any rate, the divine was powerful and strong. But was it also *good*? Life brought fortune and misfortune in a colourful mixture. The ancients' notions of God were thus often interwoven with fear: what if the divine is upset with me? People felt that they were not the authors of their own lives and that their lives were like a candle in the wind. It could blow out at any moment and was threatened in many ways. They could not influence the weather nor the fertility of their

"No scientific discovery has ever moved me away from faith. Everything I have learned from scientific knowledge has only led me deeper into wonder and to gratitude to my Creator.

Christoph Cardinal Schönborn (*1945) Archbishop of Vienna

soils. And where did the dead go? People felt that they were in the hands of higher powers. They often tried to influence these powers through sacrifice; they told themselves: If we give God the best we have, He will favour us. And so they sacrificed fruits, animals, even people to God (or the gods) – an arrangement that was supposed to be mutual.

The people of Israel obviously had a special instinct for divine things. When we read the Old Testament, we become part of an exemplary story of *learning about God*. We see Israel bid farewell to the polytheism of the ancient Orient.
God can only be one.

Y **Question 30:** Why do we believe in only one God?

Sun, moon and stars, still worshipped as gods by neighbouring peoples, were ridiculed as lamps in the sky by the Bible. Abraham learns that this one God is approachable. And he learns that this God doesn't want any human sacrifices. In the Psalms it says: "For you have no delight in sacrifice; if I were to give a burnt-offering, you would not be pleased" (Ps 51:16). But what obviously pleases God is a "clean heart" (Ps 51:10). Being good, being righteous apparently has something to do with a God who is good and righteous in himself. So, how does evil come into the world then? Where do hatred and violence, guilt and death, children's tears, the suffering of innocent animals come from?

Psalm 51

Question 357: Is atheism always a sin against the First Commandment?

ATHEISM

AGNOSTICISM

Today, a distinction is made between three ways of relating to God: atheism, agnosticism and theism. ATHEISM (which came late in human history) consists in the supposed certainty that God does not exist. AGNOSTICISM starts from the premise that we cannot know anything certain about God; therefore one does not have to deal with religion at all.

> The probability of life originating from accident is comparable to the probability of the Unabridged Dictionary resulting from an explosion in a printing factory.
>
> **Edwin G. Conklin** (1863–1952), US-Biologist

THEISM starts out from the existence of God, while not yet saying what that is - "God". A principle, a feeling, a universal reason, a spirit, a person, a kind of cosmic energy?

When **CS Lewis** (1898-1963), the author of the "Chronicles of Narnia", became a Christian, he was already a *theist*. Through reflection, Lewis came to the realisation that God had to exist. But it did not touch him. It was just a cold, inconsequential assumption. How could one get in touch with this vast other side of reality? To CS Lewis it seemed impossible. He felt like Hamlet, a character in a William Shakespeare play – like someone who plays a role in a play he didn't write himself. But one day he had this decisive insight: "If Hamlet and Shakespeare should ever meet, it had to happen at Shakespeare's instigation. Hamlet could not initiate anything." So one could also say: The essence of Christianity is that the author of the play unexpectedly enters the stage and shows himself to his characters, i.e. that the unfathomable God emerges from his mystery and shows himself the way he is. We call this REVELATION.

! "The Atheist Bus Campaign" (Photo above) was a campaign initiated in 2008 by British journalist Ariane Sherine. It was supported by Richard Dawkins.

Question 7: Why did God have to show himself in order for us to be able to know what he is like?

REVELATION

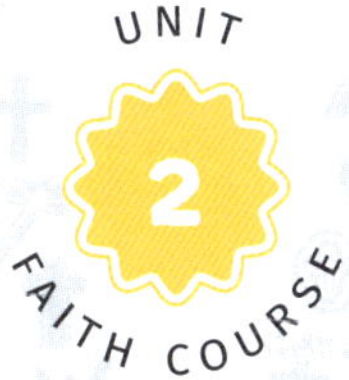

How does God show himself to human beings?

THIS UNIT TALKS ABOUT

how the immensely great God
enters our limited minds
and why this becomes
easier to understand through
a perfectly normal love story
than through
thick books.

Question 6: Can we grasp God at all in concepts?

Anyone who has ever experienced a love story in their life knows this exciting moment. Someone you really like being with is humming and hawing, struggling with themselves, blushing: "I ... I have something to tell you!" Your heart is in your mouth. You suspect what is coming next: the person who loves you is taking a huge risk because you could laugh at them and scorn them. But they take the risk; they *reveal themselves to you* and let you look into the deepest recesses of their heart. If they didn't take this risk, you would never know how they feel about you.

Question 4: Can we know the existence of God by our reason?

Just as there is no love story without revelation, there is also no knowledge of God without God emerging from the depths of his concealment and revealing himself, that is, he makes himself understandable with regards to what he's like and what his intentions are for us. God is much too great for us to define and conceptualise him. How ridiculous is any attempt to contain him within some formula! As the great philosopher Augustine said, "*Si comprehendis, non est Deus*" – which freely translated means: If you have understood him, then what you think you have understood definitely isn't God! Actually, we should put it like Karl Bath did: "God is known only by God." A Christmas beetle cannot cope with infinitesimal calculus either, after all!

Augustine (354–430) was one of the greatest Christian philosophers – and also a Saint. He has a hell of a life story! Before he was baptised he lived in sin and had a son. Later he became a bishop.

How could God show Himself to us so that we can understand? With a neon sign on the horizon? Or would SciFi freaks prefer it if he ascended like some extraterrestrial monster from the depths of the ocean in front of running cameras? That's ridiculous. Wouldn't we be totally blinded if God were to show himself to us directly? Therefore, God can be found *in the many traces* displaying his power and greatness, for example in *nature* and *conscience*. In *nature*: the sun rises and creation shows itself in a fullness and beauty that lets us feel: this is God's DNA. From the smallest cells

Question 295: What is conscience?

all the way to the macrocosm everything is perfectly coordinated. *Conscience* usually tells us that it is *absolutely not good* to beat a child, or to rob or cheat someone. It's like it's the voice of God that absolutely demands this of us. If we ignore it, we feel like we can never again show our face to this mysterious authority within us.

God is present much more intensively than in vague experiences of nature. He is the highlight, the joke, *the punch line in your life*. Many people have no idea of this; they believe that the question of meaning in life can also be answered without God. They are punching well below their weight if they think a meaningful life is all about getting the maximum fun out of life before being buried in the local cemetery.

Y **Question 45:** Do natural laws and natural systems come from God also?

Y **Question 50:** What role do we play in God's providence?

> Only where God is seen does life truly begin. Only when we meet the living God in Christ do we know what life is. We are not some casual and meaningless product of evolution. Each of us is the result of a thought of God. Each of us is willed, each of us is loved, each of us is necessary.

Pope Benedict XVI, 2005

Question 43: Is the world a product of chance?

The faith experience is like the five minutes before your grand love story begins that turns your life upside down: everything is grey, then he or she comes around the corner and it's a whole new world for you! This is how it is with faith. Your Creator, your Lord and Redeemer comes around the corner, and from then on you have a common story. The adventure begins. Later you will say: I had no idea what life really is!

What is a human being? Someone whispers to me: *She* knew Albert Einstein, *he* was on stage with Michael Jackson, the Prime Minister loves having a meal with *him*. And what about a being that's never been in the spotlight? The child on the edge of the south Sahara? The old man with dementia, saliva running down his chin? Are those two worth less? Do we care about them merely out of a certain sentimentality? Nowhere in the kingdom of the spirit, in any religion does the human being have greater importance than in Judaism and Christianity. Here the human being – *every* human being – is "crowned with glory and honour" (Ps 8:5), "in the image of God" (Gen 1:27), the being whom God looks upon with everlasting love, the one who can speak with God eye to eye. "Your eyes beheld my unformed substance." (Ps 139:16). A new quality of humane existence begins with *God's revelation*.

Y **Question 280:** What reasons do Christians give for human dignity?

Y **Question 56:** Do human beings have a special place in creation?

Ps 8; Gen 1

Ps 139

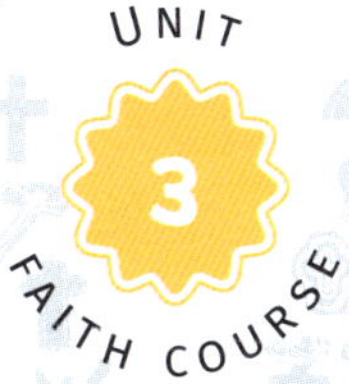

What does faith mean?

THIS UNIT TALKS ABOUT

whether you want to
live your life alone
or whether you believe there is
someone
who knows all your paths
and is glad when you
are heading in his direction.

What do you need for your everyday life? Lots of faith. I have no proof that Tonga really exists. Nevertheless, I trust the website. I believe that I will land in Nukualofa if I book a ticket and go to the airport. There are very few things in life that we can prove. And if someone says to his girlfriend: "Prove that you love me," then you can be pretty sure that this love is over before it has started.

Question 12: How can we tell what belongs to the true faith?

Whenever someone talks about faith, someone comes around the corner and says, disparagingly: *"Faith means not knowing."* What it means is that faith is more for naive types: people with intelligence are the ones that know things. The rumour going around regarding the Church is that her entire existence is based on

Question 21: Faith – What is it?

largely unproven assumptions. People are expected *to believe*. You'll no longer be burnt at the stake for it if you know better, but it's still a bit heretical when someone says: 'God?... Well, for me that's more like a kind of original formula.' And doesn't that have some justification? If God is as important as religions always claim he is, then they should use their brains to get to the point of this nebulous term. We'd like to hear something like: $e^{i\pi}$+ 1 = God. Something like that. Then we would have clear proof at hand and wouldn't have to stuff around with 'faith'. Then we'd know!

Let's say the formula is right. We would know! What would happen after its publication in the *Physical Review*? Would people convert, get down on their knees and worship this wonderful formula? I'll bet the answer is No! The people would say: Aha! And they would tuck it away in a remote region of the brain along with the law of gravity. No one would do like the 49 Christians did in the year 304, when they were dragged before the Emperor Diocletian. The 49 had been interrogated in Carthage, because they had been caught attending Mass. They were given one last chance: they could renounce their God and for appearances sake pay a little homage to the emperor. They didn't do that, but said, "We can't live without the Sunday." That cost them their lives.

Question 32: What does it mean to say that God is truth?

1.7: Why should I believe in God?

So, faith seems to be about something much more precious than being informed about certain facts. Let's put it this way: It is not about *knowledge of God*, but about *relationship with* God. Let's take an extreme example. Someone comes and says to my face: "Your mother is a slut!" I am utterly outraged by this, although I have not accompanied my mother at every turn for the last 50 years, so in fact I cannot prove that my mother is the most loving and faithful person in the world. There is a deep *relationship of trust* between my mother and me, and I would never

Question 454: How strongly obligatory is the truth of the faith?

Question 20: How can we respond to God when he speaks to us?

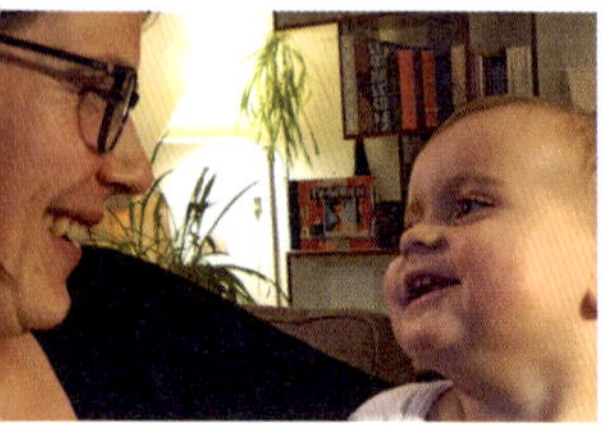

let my mother's memory be tarnished. When it comes to God too, the *relationship of trust* is the be-all and end-all. By the way, the word FAITH comes from the Indo-European root *leubh* – which means something like 'to love', 'to declare dear', 'to endorse', 'to praise'.

FAITH

And that's exactly the point. To believe means to love God, to say that God is loving, to endorse God, to praise God. When more and more young people today discover *joyful praise*, they are at the fiery heart of faith. At any rate, they are closer than the clever ones looking for the Absolute in libraries.

Y **Question 22:** How does one go about believing?

To believe as a Christian means in fact to entrust oneself to the meaning that upholds me and the world, taking it as the firm ground on which I can fearlessly stand
Pope Benedict XVI

In speaking of human things, we say that it is necessary to know them before we can love them... in speaking of divine things it is necessary to love them in order to know them

Blaise Pascal (1623–1662), Mathematician and philosopher

Faith is not an invention of the Church. If it is an invention, it is Jesus' invention. Again and again, in John's Gospel he says: "Whoever believes in me..." – well, what? – "... has eternal life" (Jn 6:47) , and "... even though they die, they will live" (Jn 11:25), and they, "... will also do the works that I do and, in fact, will do greater works than these" (Jn 14:12).

Strong stuff! As a matter of course, Jesus refers *believing* to himself. I was always surprised that nobody protested when Jesus said: "I am the way, and the truth, and the life" (Jn 14:6). *I am*! He doesn't say: I know a way, I know the truth, I have some experience of life. No. *I am*! Basically, Jesus leaves us with only two possibilities: either *I believe him* and put all my eggs in this basket, or I believe he is the Donald Trump of religion. "Faith," says Pope Benedict "means leaving things up to God."

Y **Question 71:** Why are the reports about Jesus called "the Gospel", the "Good news"?

” If the saints in heaven could return to earth once more, they would be inflamed with love, and would be tirelessly concerned with spreading the faith across the entire world, with a view to proclaiming God's infinite love to all humankind. For the saints know much more than anyone on earth how much the Father, Son and Holy Spirit are worthy of being known. After all, they are enraptured when they see the glory that is the reward in heaven for any act, even the smallest of them, that spreads the faith.

St Vincent Pallotti (1795–1850)

What is the Bible good for?

This unit talks about

a hidden treasure,

a book you should read every day,

because it has more content

than a thousand how-to books and more substance

than any other book

in the world.

hen monks created this beautiful initial letter, Sacred Scripture for ordinary people in the Church was still forbidden. Isn't that crazy? "Not knowing Scripture means not knowing Christ," said Jerome, one of the early Church Fathers. How did that happen? Simple Christians did not read the Bible; they heard it only during church services, in small doses, with church commentary.

Question 17: What significance does the Old Testament have for Christians?

Question 18: What significance does the New Testament have for Christians?

The Dominican monk and inquisitor **Melchor Cano** is like a figure out of "The Name of the Rose". In 1559,

when a Spanish bishop demanded the translation of the Bible into the national language, Cano stepped in and warned that things would end up as they had in Germany, where Martin Luther had translated the Bible into German 40 years earlier. The Bible, he said, was not for "carpenter's wives": "Even if these women demand with insatiable appetites to eat of this fruit, it is necessary to forbid it and place a fiery knife in front of them so that the people cannot reach it." Also Teresa of Avila, the great Church reformer of the 16th century, was also affected by this and was in great distress because of it. But one night she was comforted by a vision: "The Lord told me, 'Be not distressed, for I will give you *a living book*.'"

What would happen if we treated the Bible like we treat our cell phone? If we always carried it with us; or at least the small pocket-sized Gospel, what would happen? What would happen if we turned back when we forget it, if we opened it more times a day, if we read the message of God contained in the Bible the way we read messages on our cellphones?

Pope Francis

The attack of the inquisitor Melchor Cano should be seen less as a document oppressing women but more an assault on the people. Women then, just as they are now, were more interested in religion than men. Women – perhaps he thought – would read and discuss the Bible enthusiastically; and if then on top of that they were influenced by the Reformation, a new Church would spring up on every street corner. It is well known that Luther had established the *Sola Scriptura* principle: a Christian only needs the Holy Scriptures and not the interpretations of the priests as well. The Bible was self-explanatory. In fact, even in Luther's times, the Reformation movement was already entangled in a plethora of different interpretations. Everyone wanted to follow the Bible. But in fact, some of them followed the interpretation of Calvin, others the interpretation of Zwingli, others again the interpretation of Thomas Müntzer or John Knox ...

Y **Question 130:** Are non-Catholic Christians our sisters and brothers also?

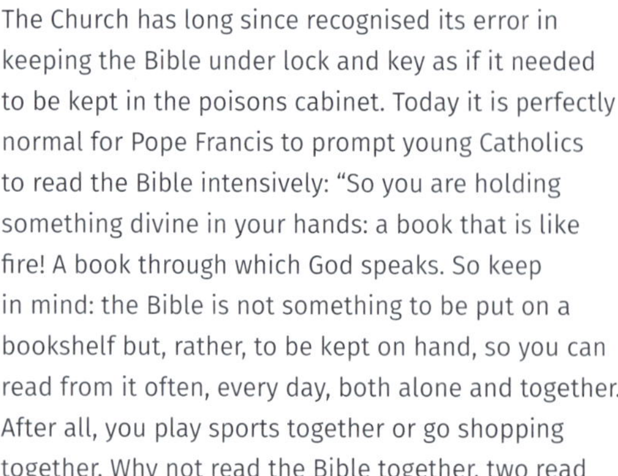

The Church has long since recognised its error in keeping the Bible under lock and key as if it needed to be kept in the poisons cabinet. Today it is perfectly normal for Pope Francis to prompt young Catholics to read the Bible intensively: "So you are holding something divine in your hands: a book that is like fire! A book through which God speaks. So keep in mind: the Bible is not something to be put on a bookshelf but, rather, to be kept on hand, so you can read from it often, every day, both alone and together. After all, you play sports together or go shopping together. Why not read the Bible together, two read together, three or four at a time? Outdoors in nature, in the woods, on the beach, in the evening, by the light of a few candles? You will have a powerful experience!" But of course it needs to be said: it is part of the Church's history of guilt that for centuries it did not allow simple folk to draw from the riches of God's word.

Question 16: What is the right way to read the Bible?

Yet the Church did not abandon one principle: *The Bible is the Book of the Church*. It has grown out of its life; it is and remains her heart chamber. "We should never read Scripture alone," says Pope Benedict. "We find too many doors closed and could easily slip into error. The Bible has been written by the People of God and for the People of God under the inspiration of the Holy Spirit" We must not forget our living connection with the Church, that is, we must not make ourselves masters of the Bible. "The devil can cite the Scripture for his purpose" Shakespeare once said.

Question 19: What role does Sacred Scripture play in the Church?

But what exactly is the word of God? Everything that God has to say to us he has told us in Jesus Christ. He is the Revelation of revelations and the actual Word of God. We gain access to the word of God in writing

1.14: What is the difference between the Bible and the Koran?

through *Scripture* and orally through the *Apostolic (or oral) Tradition*. It is easy to picture this: up until the year 397 – when the Synod of Carthage determined which books belonged to the Holy Scriptures – generations of Christians lived virtually without the New. Testament. Were they living, therefore, without the "Word of God"? No, the Word was alive in them, "living and active, sharper than any two-edged sword" (Heb 4:12). Otherwise they would not have survived the catacombs and the cruel Colosseum games of antiquity.

Y **Question 10:** With Jesus Christ has everything been said, or does Revelation continue even after him?

Heb 4:12

Read the Gospel and read it again and again, without ceasing, to have more and more the Spirit, the deeds, the words, the thoughts of Jesus before your eyes, to think, speak, act like Jesus, to follow the example and instructions of Jesus!

Bl. Charles de Foucauld (1858–1916)

What does it mean to say that God becomes man?

THIS UNIT TALKS ABOUT

perhaps the most objectionable element
in all of Christianity,
that is, that for over 2000 years,
the Church has held to the belief
that God became as human
as any baby that is being born.

Question 9: What does God show us about himself when he sends his Son to us?

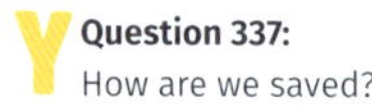

Question 337: How are we saved?

Jean-Paul Sartre, French philosopher (1905–1980), was, next to Sigmund Freud, the second most epochal atheist and anti-Christian of the 20th century. The late quite bitter and radical Sartre wanted to belong to those who made of God "an outdated hypothesis that will peacefully die off by itself." But it was Sartre of all people who – perhaps better than any theologian – explained what God's becoming man is all about. Theology speaks of the "INCARNATION" (the becoming flesh) of God. Why did God want to become flesh, of all things?

INCARNATION 

(from Lat. *caro, carnis* = flesh, becoming flesh): God's Incarnation in Jesus Christ. This is the foundation of the Christian faith and of the hope of humankind's salvation.

It is hard to believe that **Sartre** wrote a nativity play, *Bariona* or *the Son of Thunder*. Sartre wrote and staged it in 1940 when he was a prisoner of war near Trier. The play was intended for the camp Christmas party. For Sartre, this time in Trier was emotionally moving. He delved into Catholic authors like Paul Claudel and Georges Bernanos ("The two great discoveries I made in the prison camp were *The Satin Slipper* and the *Diary of a Country Priest*. They are the only books that have made a really deep impression on me"), met some priests and felt "a sense of brotherhood" with them: "I found a form of collective life that I hadn't come across since the *École Normale*, and in short I want to say I was happy there." Sartre almost dealt with the hole he felt in his being and the absence of his father. But he wasn't to go that far. Yet at least he wrote "Bariona" as something that would ensure "the broadest unity between Christians and non-believers."

" Do what God did: become a human being!

Bishop Franz Kamphaus (*1932), formerly bishop of Limburg

> "By nature incomprehensible and inaccessible, he was invisible and unthinkable, but now he wished to be understood, to be seen and thought of.
>
> **St Bernard of Clairvaux** (ca. 1090–1153)

The play contains a breath-taking passage in which Sartre explains his own godlessness. He has Bariona say: "A God-Man, a God made of our humble flesh, a God who would agree to know the taste of the salt in our throats when the whole world abandons us, a God who would accept in advance to suffer what I suffer today... Let's be gone, it's folly!" Elsewhere he has Bariona say that if God were to become man for his sake he "should love him to the exclusion of all others. It would be as if there were a blood bond between him and me and I would not find it too much to give my life out of gratitude." Bariona is not ungrateful. "But what God would be foolish enough to do that? Not ours, certainly. He has always shown himself to be proud."

Question 76: Why did God become incarnate in Jesus?

Question 33: What does it mean to say that God is love?

Question 402: What is love?

> God is so great that he can become small. God is so powerful that he can make himself vulnerable and come to us as a defenceless child, so that we can love him.

Pope Benedict XVI 24-12-2005

And Sartre's Mary says: "This God is my baby. This divine flesh is my flesh. He's made of me, he has my eyes and this shape of his mouth is the same shape as mine. He looks like me. He's God and he looks like me ..."

And no woman has had her God just for herself that way. A tiny little God you can take in your arms and cover with kisses, a God all warm and smiling and breathing, a God you can touch, who's alive.

Question 82: Isn't it improper to call Mary the "Mother" of God?

Question 13: Can the Church err in questions of faith?

MONOPHYSITISM

SUBORDINATIONISM

ADOPTIONISM

DOCETISM

No sentence in the Holy Scriptures has caused more scandal within and beyond the Church than John 1:14: "And the Word (= God) *became flesh* and lived among us." For the Greeks so much in love with the spirit, and who had just disposed of their absurd pantheon, this was simply shocking. And even in the Church, one heresy after another attacked it. The *Monophysites* taught that Christ was not true man and true God at the same time; he only possessed the divine nature. The *Subordinationists* taught that Jesus was a kind of second-class god, not on a level with the Father and the Holy Spirit. The *Adoptionists* taught that Christ was only a man. At the baptism in the Jordan, God had, as it were, "adopted" him as his Son. The *Docetists*, on the other hand, taught that Christ had truly been the Son of God, but that he did not have a real body and therefore only seemingly died on the cross.

Nestorius, Bishop and Patriarch of Constantinople in the 5th century, was removed from office at the Council of Ephesus because he insisted that he could not recognise "a two or three-month-old God." The Church has always maintained that Jesus of Nazareth, born of the Virgin Mary, is "true man and true God at the same time." And that hasn't always been easy!

Y **Question 77:** What does it mean to say that Christ is at the same time true God and true man?

Either this man was, and is, the Son of God, or else a madman or something worse. You can shut him up for a fool, you can spit at him and kill him as a demon or you can fall at his feet and call him Lord and God, but let us not come with any patronising nonsense about his being a great human teacher. He has not left that open to us. He did not intend to.

English writer **CS Lewis** on Jesus

Imagine if I had to worship a God who had kept himself out of the dirt of this earth! I would immediately become an atheist. But I know that what Sartre longed for is true – "a God one can touch and who lives." God has a human face.

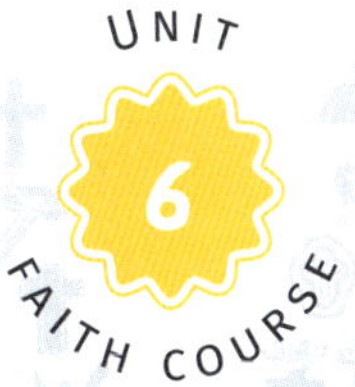

Why is there suffering?

THIS UNIT TALKS ABOUT

the sufferings of the poor,
the pains of the sick
and children's tears;
that no theology can be indifferent
to this without disgracing itself
and showing itself in a bad light.

A young couple are looking forward to their baby. The child is born. It has no arms. Why does God allow this? I once goaded an old priest regarding a series of catastrophes that had taken place near me. He just kept shaking his head and said only one sentence in a quiet voice, "God doesn't make mistakes." I gulped and could not reconcile myself with this for a long time. Later I met the mother of a child with Down's syndrome. She told me: "We wouldn't want to exchange Felix for any other child in the world. He is the darling of our family ..."

THEODICY 

The word *theodicy* (Greek: in defence of God) has been around since **GW Leibniz** (1646–1716). It concerns the question of how a good God can be reconciled with the suffering in the world. Everyone has to deal with suffering of this kind, whether they think God is involved or not. A *non-believer* might think that life is a game of chance where some just have bad luck. That can't be, the Christian says, because a single child's tears would reduce the meaning of the universe to dust unless there is someone who "will wipe every tear from their eyes" (Rev 21:4). Yet even Christians have no infallible formula in their pockets to whisk away suffering and prove the goodness of God. Like other people, Christians are at a loss given the incomprehensible variation of the misery of innocent people. Not only do people suffer, but also animals; in a sense, all creation suffers. Nevertheless, Christians believe that life is worthwhile, that every life God gives is worthwhile. But they have to put up with gloating remarks like: "Where was your God when this or that happened?" What do they do then?

Y **Question 66:** Was it part of God's plan for people to suffer and die?

 **Rev 21:4**

They pass the question on to God, sometimes in tears, sometimes with a slightly rebellious undertone, as Romano Guardini (1885–1968) did: "Why, God, these fearful detours on the way to salvation, the suffering of the innocent, why sin?" By the way, Guardini also said that he would not only let himself be asked questions at the Last Judgement, but would also ask questions himself.

Question 240: How was "sickness" interpreted in the Old Testament?

 **Ps 10**

This is by no means a godless approach. Even the Bible does not keep suffering well away from God. People often engage in a quite unsettling dialogue with their God, even accusing him: "Why O Lord do you stand far off? Why do you hide yourself in times of trouble?" (Ps 10:1). Then there is poor Job from whom absolutely everything has been taken: "I cry to you and you do not answer me; I stand and you merely

> In suffering, man experiences the power of God, in acting he relies too much on himself and becomes weak. In suffering he is purified and therefore wise and prudent.
>
> **St John Henry Cardinal Newman** (1801–1890)

 **Job**

look at me" (Job 30:20). And what does God say? "My thoughts are not your thoughts, nor are your ways my ways, says the LORD" (Is 55:8). Does he not even care about us? Does God really not make mistakes?

Question 40: Can God do anything? Is he almighty?

The question of God and suffering remains a mystery, surrounded, of course, by a number of certainties. We know God is almighty, otherwise he would not be God.

Question 51: If God is all-knowing and all-powerful why does he not prevent evil?

Justifiably, that there is evil and suffering seems to us to be a malfunction, discontinuation, something that simply shouldn't be. Sacred Scripture sees the world as fundamentally poisoned by evil, the author of which is not and cannot be God. God is the enemy of evil; he thinks "plans for welfare and not for harm" (Jer 29:11). In Isaiah it even says: "As a mother comforts her child, so I will comfort you" (Is 66:13).

 **Jer 29:11**

 **Is 66:13**

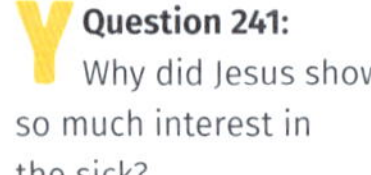

In the end, the threads only come together in Jesus. In his Son, God himself enters into the suffering of his creation, up to the radical point where the dying Son yells at his Father: "My God, my God, why have you forsaken me?" (Mk 15:34). What sounds like the most disturbing of divine accusations is in truth the incredible Psalm 22, only half of which is the cry of one who feels betrayed, while the other half is a unique hymn of praise to the God who saves: "For he did not despise or abhor the affliction of the afflicted. He did not hide his face from me, but heard when I cried to him" (Ps 22:25) The Father does not leave his son in death; he awakens him to new life – and with him, all who believe in him. And thus Paul says: "We know that all things work together for good for those who love God" (Rom 8:28).

 **Mk 15:34**

 **Ps 22**

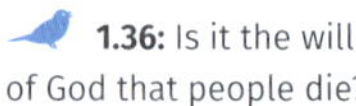

 **Rom 8:28**

> „God, whose very own you are, will lead you safely through all things; and when you cannot stand it, God will carry you in His arms.
>
> **Francis de Sales** (1567–1622)

“I believe that God can and will bring good out of evil” Protestant theologian **Dietrich Bonhoeffer** (1906–1945) once said. He wrote this in the death cell which the Nazis had sent him to as a resistance fighter. There, four months before his execution (and therefore facing death) he wrote a poem that he sent to his fiancée:

With every power for good to stay and guide me,
Comforted and inspired beyond all fear...
Should it be ours to drain the cup of grieving
Even to the dregs of pain, at Thy command,
We will not falter, thankfully receiving
All that is given by Thy loving hand.

Question 49: Does God guide the world and my life?

Why the cross?

This unit talks about

the question of why,
of all things,
Christians have made
one of the
most brutal instruments of torture
in antiquity their trademark,
and why
they are so ready to kneel
before the suffering
of a convicted criminal.

Question 51: If God is all-knowing and all-powerful, why does he not prevent evil?

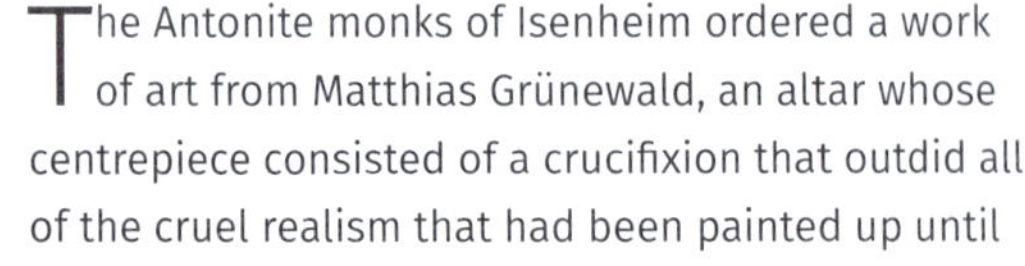

The Antonite monks of Isenheim ordered a work of art from Matthias Grünewald, an altar whose centrepiece consisted of a crucifixion that outdid all of the cruel realism that had been painted up until

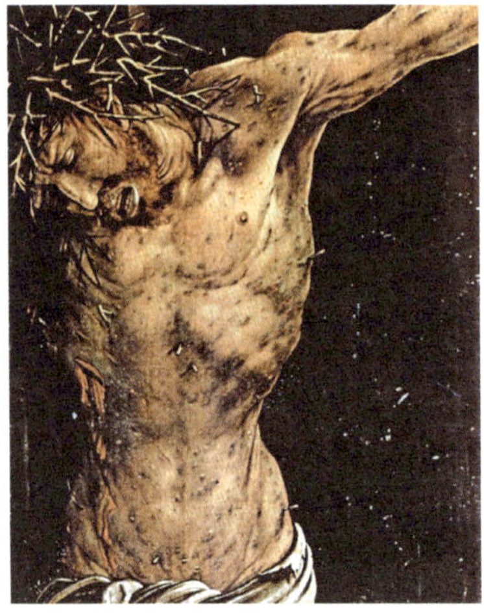

then: hands in agony, an emaciated body, only skin and bones, pitted with festering ulcers and pus, thorns piercing the head, blood and cuts without number. The friars set up the altar in the chapel and each day they brought the incurably ill to this picture. They had to look to someone feverish, writhing in pain, or someone suffering the plague, covered in blue-black lumps, just as if their own body had been nailed to the wood. The Antonites considered prayer in front of this cross to be *quasi-medicina* – a kind of medicine. Were they mocking the poorest of the poor? Do we really have to show sufferers their own misery?

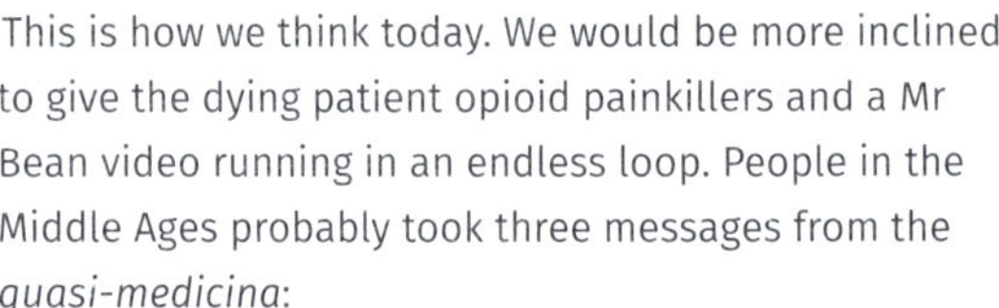

This is how we think today. We would be more inclined to give the dying patient opioid painkillers and a Mr Bean video running in an endless loop. People in the Middle Ages probably took three messages from the *quasi-medicina*:

> He himself bore our sins in his body on the cross, so that, free from sins, we might live for righteousness; by his wounds you have been healed.
>
> **1 Pet 2:24**

1. The message of God's empathy with them,
2. The message: Repent your sins,
3. The message of hope for fundamental salvation.
What sounds cruel at first sight deserves a closer look:

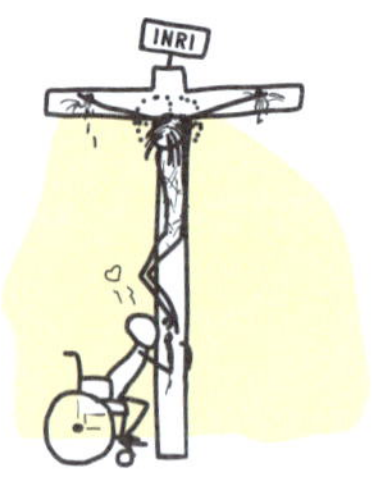

1. When someone is suffering greatly, the deepest pain is often the feeling of being abandoned by God and humans both. I have to go through it alone! It is comforting when other sufferers are nearby. And it is doubly comforting when God is there. What would I do in an emergency with a God who is surrounded by blissful spirits but has never suffered what I am suffering! In former times people used to say: *offer*

up your sufferings with the sufferings of Christ! Translated into modern language this means: Transform your suffering into a gift for others, do it together with Jesus, who suffered for you on the cross, who gave you his death as a gift for your salvation and the salvation of the whole world.

Question 102: Why are we too supposed to accept suffering in our lives and "take up our cross" and thereby follow Jesus?

> Christ's cross is like the wings of a bird, which are indeed borne by the creature, and yet support her flight towards heaven.

St Bernard of Clairvaux (ca. 1090–1153)

2. Anyone who knows people who are facing death often learns that mental pain is the greater pain: the pain of not being able to undo one's life: the wounds one has inflicted, the people one has abandoned or whom we have failed one way or another. In remorse about an imperfect, often broken life, looking to someone who makes up for everything, who also wants to make my story, too, an absolutely positive story, is comforting. Even if it is our last moment: "In the cross is salvation, in the cross is life, in the Cross is hope" (Good Friday liturgy).

Question 229: What prepares a person for repentance?

3. Christians often die holding a cross in their hands or in sight of the cross. With Jesus you can see clearly ... to life's punchline – and that does not consist of interment, burial at sea or cremation. The final punchline of life is the resurrection from the dead. "True revolution, the revolution that radically transforms life was brought about by Jesus Christ through his Resurrection," says Pope Francis.

Question 108: What changed in the world as a result of the Resurrection?

> The everlasting God has in his wisdom foreseen from eternity the cross that He now presents to you as a gift from His inmost Heart. This cross He now sends you He has considered with His all-knowing eyes, understood with His divine mind, tested with His wise justice, warmed with loving arms and weighed with His own hands to see that it be not one inch too large and not one ounce too heavy for you. He has blessed it with His Holy Name, anointed it with His consolation, taken one last glance at you and your courage, and then sent it to you from heaven, a special greeting from God to you, an alms of the All-Merciful Love of God.

St Francis de Sales (1567–1622)

ALMS ➡
a merciful offering

Question 136: How does the Church view other religions?

The question of how to escape suffering is asked in all religions on earth. We may also ask them about dying. Imagine if the Antonites, instead of a cross from Meister Grünewald, had acquired a Buddha so they could assemble the sick before his smiling peace of mind. Buddhism puts it succinctly: "To live is to suffer" and this suffering does not cease until we have weaned ourselves off the cause of all suffering, our appetites (= desires). But I do not want to be perfectly happy, I want to achieve the deepest goal of my desires: to be completely whole. I want to have life, life in abundance, life without end. I do not want to wean myself off life, don't want to count down all my joys until they are all used up. I'm a Christian; whatever hardship I am suffering I know I will come through it okay.

I came that they may have life, and have it abundantly.

Jn 10:10

"A person without religion," Archbishop Helder Camara once said: "is a wanderer without a destination, a questioner without an answer, a wrestler without victory and a dying person without new life." Archbishop Camara might well have said: "... without the Christian Religion." The more crosses are removed from classrooms, courtrooms, and from mountain peaks, the more Christians must regard the image of the crucified they have in their hearts as holy, for it is an image before the great picture of joy, the rising of the sun: the resurrection.

Question 281: Why do we yearn for happiness?

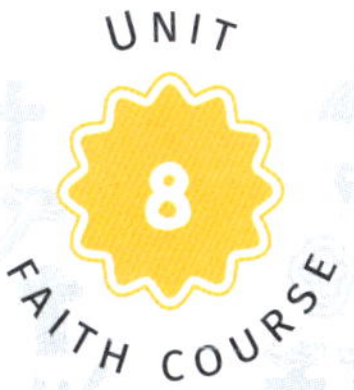

Why do we need the Church?

THIS UNIT TALKS ABOUT

what the Church is:

something external and a secret

both human and divine at the same time.

A stream through which

true life flows to us.

A place to share love.

A home in joy.

Question 121: What does "Church" mean?

If you want to understand the innermost mystery of the Church, look at this picture: at first glance - a picture of Mary. Since the earliest times, Mary has been considered the archetype of the Church. Why? Her body was the first dwelling place for God when he became human. Moreover, for Mary, Jesus was the whole purpose of her life. She was around him – he was in her. It should be the same with the Church: a place where the Risen One can live. A place of perfect love and willingness. Like when God came knocking at a young woman's door in Galilee. God was looking for a place to be in the world. "Your will be done," Mary told God's angel.

Lk 1:38

Question 128: What does it mean to say that the Church is the "Temple of the Holy Spirit"?

It wasn't only then that God was looking for a place where Jesus could lead his life. He is still looking for a place for him among us today. This is why we say that the Church is the "*Temple of the Holy Spirit*". The word "temple" means something like "holy space".

While God is present everywhere, it is often difficult to distinguish where we are dealing with something divine and where we are dealing with something purely human. It's fascinating when we read in Scripture that God really wants to "live" among us. Making God "at home" with us is our common task. But we are not the ones who are supposed to build a temple. Many have worked on that. Ultimately it is God himself, the Holy Spirit, who has been and is still building God's dwelling place among us, day and night.

And they shall know that I am the LORD their God, who brought them out of the land of Egypt that I might dwell among them; I am the LORD their God.
Ex 29:46

The Church has no other purpose in life than Jesus himself. We just need to be there – around Jesus – and let him work. Then we are the Church. In the Gospel of Luke Jesus once said, "My mother and my brothers are those who hear the word of God and do it" (Lk 8:21). "The Church," says Pope Benedict XVI, "is God's family in the world." So, the Church first of all is the living Jesus, and only then becomes his "family", we sinners,

2.1 What is the Church? Who belongs to the Church?

Lk 8:21

the imperfect ones, who are allowed to be "one body" with Jesus.

Question 126: What does it mean to say that the Church is "the Body of Christ"?

Yes, Jesus got so deeply involved with us that we are, as it were, "one body" with him. This is testified to by the Holy Scriptures in many places. St. Augustine (350–430) has profound things to say about what happens when we receive Holy Communion: "Receive what you are, the *Body of Christ*, that you may become what you receive, the *Body of Christ*."

I will make of you a great nation, and I will bless you, and make your name great, so that you will be a blessing. **Gen 12:2**

An ancient biblical image of the Church was revived at the Second Vatican Council, the image of the (*new*) "*People of God*" a people that "presses forward amid the persecutions of the world and the consolations of God." The ancient people of God meant the people of Israel, with whom God had walked a long way. Without forgetting the people of Israel, Jesus Christ has now created a new people for himself that takes people from all nations and cultures with him on the way to God.

When we look at the Church today, we are overwhelmed by what it has become over two thousand years. We could easily lose track. Sometimes we look at the huge *institution*, see churches and cathedrals, priests and bishops, hear about Catholic Charities, finances. Then again, we look at the *spiritual reality* of the Church, hear about vocations and see people who pray or give their lives to God. Both realities belong together: the *spiritual* and the *institutional*. Without the institution, the Church could not survive in the world; she needs money to be able to help people, places to meet and people who have a specific task to carry out. But all of this would just be a dead, spiritless system if the *spiritual* – God's living reality in the Holy Spirit – were not at the heart of the Church.

Question 138: How is the one, holy, catholic and apostolic Church structured?

Question 119: What does the Holy Spirit do in the Church?

Let yourselves be built into a spiritual house.
1 Pet 2:5

Yes, it is true, the scandals of the Church are and remain a disgrace and a real issue. Nevertheless, they are not just mistakes that have accidentally cropped up and that might be eliminated with a little goodwill. Jesus was involved with ordinary people but also risky types, where he was on equal footing with the hedonistic Mary Magdalene, the corrupt tax collector Zacchaeus, an adulteress caught in the act, wicked people like Judas, who ultimately betrayed him, Peter, who denied him before the cock crowed three times. If only the pure among us were allowed to belong to the Church, then it would probably be empty. At least I would never have a chance to ever find my place in her: I know myself, I'm capable of anything.

The real Church ... is not a club for the perfect, but according to Jesus' will it is a place for ordinary people to slowly change. People who sometimes throw in the towel, who have a dubious record, who urgently need to be grabbed by the scruff of their neck and improved. Fortunately, Jesus has assured us: 'Those who are well have no need of a physician, but those who are sick; I have come to call not the righteous but sinners.' (Mk 2:17) ...

We are all a bit handicapped, after all. One has a problem with money, another with the truth, a third with sex, a fourth is unreliable, a fifth is pig-headed, then there's me, the sixth. We don't stride along in some triumphal march; we limp and hobble and creep along. But we walk together. That is the Church in which I feel at home.

Bernhard Meuser, Christsein für Einsteiger (Christianity for Beginners)

Question 123: What is the task of the Church?

The Church is not an end in itself. God does not take the slightest pleasure in her if she simply revolves around herself. He set it up for the sake of humans. It should be "a sign and instrument both of a very closely knit union with God and of the unity of the whole human race" (*Lumen Gentium*). The Church must not remain just with itself. *It must serve the people through love*: "Truly I tell you, just as you did it to one of the least of these who are members of my family, you did it to me" (Matthew 25:40)

Mt 25:40

The Church is right where it should be when it fulfils three basic tasks: *It must proclaim the Word of God*: "proclaim the message; be persistent whether the time is favourable or unfavourable; convince, rebuke, and encourage, with the utmost patience in teaching" (2 Tim 4:2). It must administer the sacraments and celebrate worship: these are the decisive places where God works on us, transforms us, liberates us and redeems us.

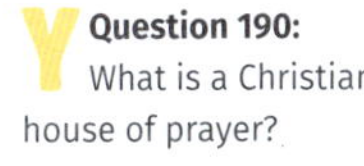

Question 190: What is a Christian house of prayer?

2 Tim 4

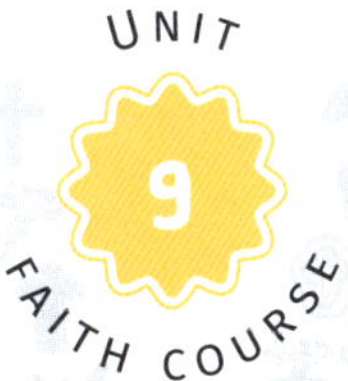

Why do Christians get baptised?

This unit talks about

the fact that normal life
ceases when it ceases.
But when we become a Christian
we get given a new life in Baptism,
a royal life that doesn't cease,
even if the world were to
end tomorrow.

Johann Wolfgang von Goethe (1749–1832) is considered the most important of the German poets.

In its time, **Goethe**'s poem "Erlkönig (usually translated as "The Elf King" in English) was a horror story. It speaks of a child in his father's arms riding "through the night dark and drear." The child becomes restless, threatened by a deadly demon, the "Elf king". The father tries to calm the desperately screaming child, clasps him even more closely to him, and urges the horse into a gallop. The ballad ends with the words: "He reaches his courtyard with toil and with dread – The child in his arms finds he motionless, dead."

Question 197: Why does the Church adhere to the practice of infant baptism?

What moves young parents when they take their baby in their arms and bring it to be baptised? It is an existential hunch that has much to do with the "Erlkönig". They have been entrusted with an innocent life. It is the deepest longing of their love to save this small child from anything that could harm it. So, they turn to God, the Lord of life, and ask for His blessing. This is baptism for so many people.

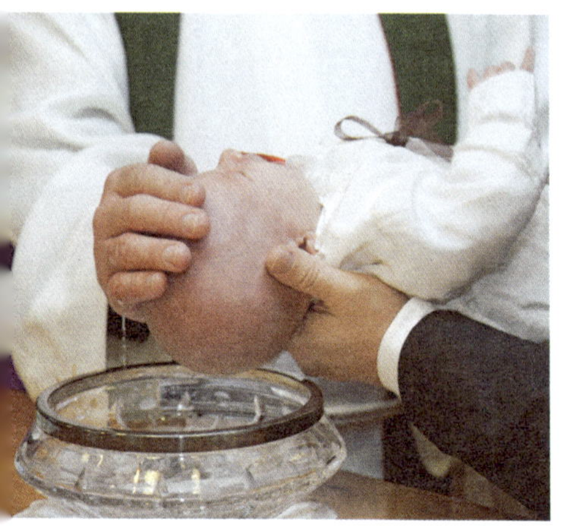

Isn't that just pious wishful thinking? What about all the mothers whose children were sent to war, never to return? Aren't we all heading for death? "The child in his arms finds he motionless, dead" – don't we have to experience this often enough? Life has its beautiful side, but we cannot really hold on to anything; everything is under threat. And because of sin we also destroy each other on top of that.

Baptism, as we have seen, is a gift; the gift of life. But a gift must be accepted, it must be lived. A gift of friendship implies a "yes" to the friend and a "no" to all that is incompatible with this friendship, to all that is incompatible with the life of God's family, with true life in Christ.

Pope Benedict XVI

Doesn't that mean that any love, any desire to protect someone (with or without divine assistance) is ultimately futile?

Question 194: What is Baptism?

Baptism must be more than a pious wish. It must be more than the ritually-charged sentimentality of uncles and aunts celebrating around a magnificently dressed baby who has no idea what is happening to it. Otherwise we might as well save ourselves the trouble!

Question 198: Who can administer Baptism?

Let's take a look at Mali. Not so long ago, a priest prepared 40 adults for baptism. During the final weeks of their three-year preparation, they were staying near the church. This did not go unnoticed. One night the priest received violent threats from militant Islamists: If these people were to be baptised, all bets were off. The priest gave the people the choice to leave. They

2.26 What are the origins of Islam?

consulted among themselves. Nobody left. One of them spoke up for them all: "We would like to be baptised – with water or with blood." They were baptised – with water. 40 adults literally risked life and limb to be baptised. And what if a militia with machine guns, jerrycans and

Baptism of blood is another word for martyrdom. Persecuted Christians in Roman times were often thrown to the lions. If not yet baptised, their martyrdom was considered as a "baptism of blood".

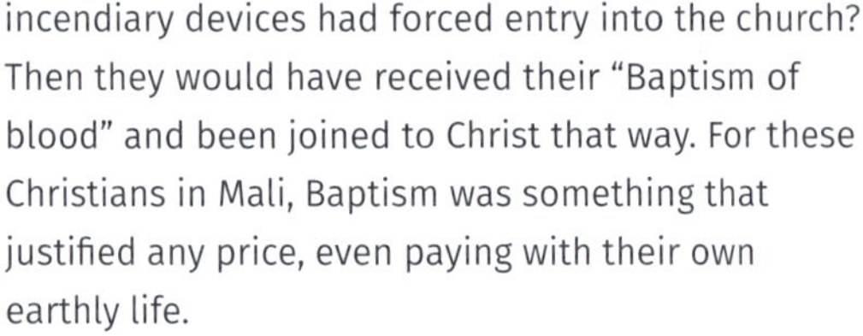

incendiary devices had forced entry into the church? Then they would have received their "Baptism of blood" and been joined to Christ that way. For these Christians in Mali, Baptism was something that justified any price, even paying with their own earthly life.

Question 195: How is Baptism administered?

* ن After the fall of Mosul in 2014, in response to the persecution of Christians and Yazidis by ISIL, an international social media campaign was launched to raise global awareness of the plight of religious minorities in Mosul, making use of the letter ن (nun) — for Nassarah ("Nazarene"), the mark that ISIL troops spray-painted on properties owned by Christians. **Wikipedia**

Mt 28:19
Mk 16:16

And they were right. *Baptism gives us everlasting life*. That is Christian teaching. The Church vouches for this. And in this she follows Jesus who demands Baptism in Mt 28:19 and, in Mk 16:16 ("The one who believes and is baptised will be saved ...") made it the gateway for entering into real life. This is the great main entrance. Of course, God also has ways for people who don't find their way to baptism. Since then, the Church has done as Peter did in the Acts of the Apostles; it calls people to faith and calls on them ceaselessly: "Repent, and be baptised every one of you in the name of Jesus Christ so that your sins may be forgiven; and you will receive the gift of the Holy Spirit" (Acts 2:38).

In 177 AD, a group of Christians was killed in Lyon, among them the deacon Sanctus. The judge asked him his name, origin and profession. To each question Sanctus always gave only one answer: "I am a Christian."

There may be people who find this bizarre: why in the world should I be connected with Jesus, even wearing him like a dress at Baptism? (Gal 3:27). The answer is simple: because Jesus is the only bridge between death and life. To make a drastic comparison: Baptism is something like the last plane out of the death zone

that was the Battle of Stalingrad.
We human beings all find ourselves in the death zone. We will not escape the doom that in large part we have brought on ourselves through sin and wickedness. But someone voluntarily comes into this death zone.

Question 200: What happens in Baptism?

In Jesus Christ, God entered the death zone to share the full measure of suffering with us human beings, to take our sins upon himself and open a way for us out of the death zone. This way out is called resurrection. Jesus was the first to die – *yet still live*.

Question 199: Is Baptism in fact the only way to salvation?

The complement to Jesus' Resurrection is Baptism. Through Baptism we are taken from the land of death into life without end. Hence we can dare to make the bold comparison: baptism is like the life-saving aircraft out of the so-called "death zone" of Stalingrad. Who says this? The Letter to the Romans: "Do you not know that all of us who have been baptised into Christ Jesus were baptised into his death? ... For if we have been united with him in a death like his, we will certainly be united with him in a resurrection like his" (Rom 6:3-5)

Rom 6:3-5

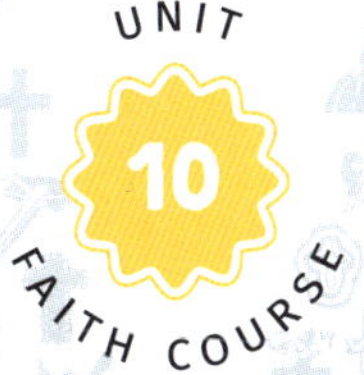

Why do Christians get confirmed?

This unit talks about

the adventure of faith.
It is the Holy Spirit
who gives you courage
and gives you the strength
to plunge in
headfirst.

There is an interesting joke regarding Confirmation: Two parish priests are discussing a bat plague in their churches: "I have really tried everything," says one priest, "I just can't get rid of them!" The other priest makes a dismissive gesture: "Nothing easier! I had them confirmed. The following day, they were all gone!"

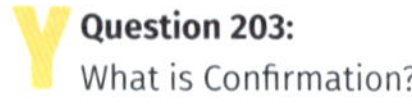

Question 203: What is Confirmation?

INITIATION
Lat: induction

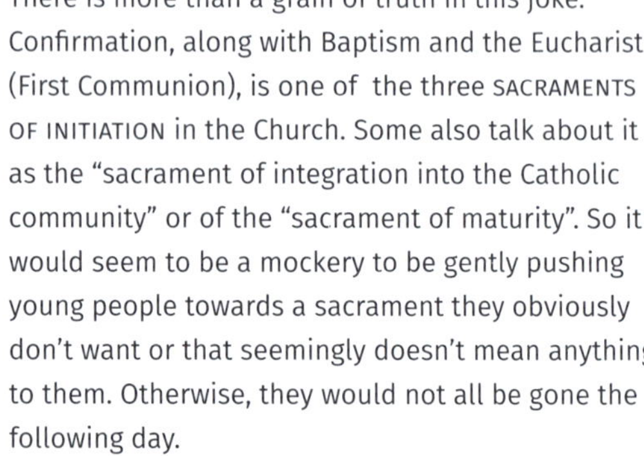

There is more than a grain of truth in this joke. Confirmation, along with Baptism and the Eucharist (First Communion), is one of the three SACRAMENTS OF INITIATION in the Church. Some also talk about it as the "sacrament of integration into the Catholic community" or of the "sacrament of maturity". So it would seem to be a mockery to be gently pushing young people towards a sacrament they obviously don't want or that seemingly doesn't mean anything to them. Otherwise, they would not all be gone the following day.

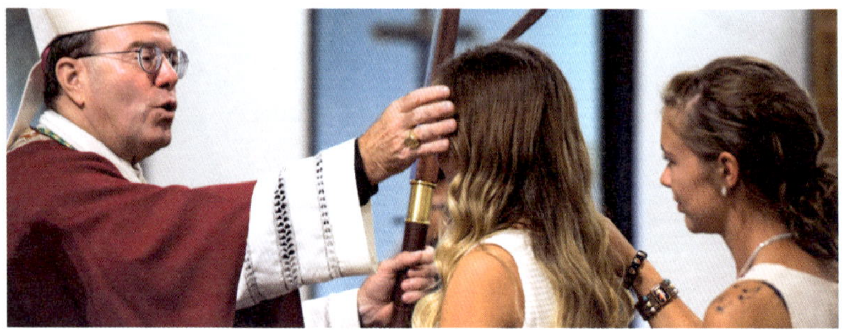

Some talk about an institutionalised "lie" and demand that this "farce" be stopped immediately. Others are more cautious and point out that one can never know how much of the Holy Spirit "sticks" where young people are concerned.

Question 204: What does Sacred Scripture say about the sacrament of Confirmation?

Clearly, we are light years away from the meaning and origin of Confirmation if we think we can't escape the mechanisms of an empty ritual.

Let's just look at the New Testament and the practice of the early Church! In Samaria, today's West Bank, people had found their way to Christ. "Now when the apostles at Jerusalem heard that Samaria had accepted the word of God, they sent Peter and John to them. The two went down and prayed for them that they might receive the Holy Spirit *(for as yet the Spirit had not come upon any of them*; they had only been baptised in the name of the Lord Jesus). Then Peter and John laid their hands on them, and they received the Holy Spirit" (Acts 8:14-17).

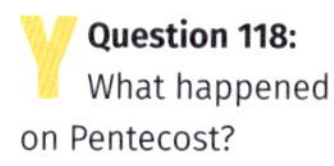

Question 118: What happened on Pentecost?

Acts 8

Paul also "confirmed". It was in the luxurious commercial city of Ephesus where he found some disciples. "He said to them, '*Did you receive the Holy Spirit when you became believers*?' They replied, 'No, we have not even heard that there is a Holy Spirit.' Then he said, 'Into what then were you baptised?' They answered, 'Into John's baptism.' Paul said, 'John baptised with the baptism of repentance, telling the people to believe in the one who was to come after him, that is, in Jesus.' On hearing this, they were baptised in the name of the Lord Jesus. When Paul had laid his hands on them, the Holy Spirit came upon them, and they spoke in tongues and prophesied – altogether there were about twelve of them" (Acts 19:2-7)

3:37 With Confirmation, does the Holy Spirit descend on us for a second time?

Acts 19

We all make sure that our children are baptised, which is good, but perhaps we're not quite so diligent in making sure they are confirmed. Without confirmation, young people remain halfway on their their journey and do not receive the Holy Spirit, who is so important in the Christian life since he gives us the strength to go on.

Pope Francis

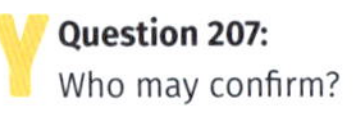

Question 207:
Who may confirm?

So what's going on? A bishop administering Confirmation once put it in popular terms: with Baptism we have a car – with Confirmation we have the fuel to run it.

> The Holy Spirit is the living presence of God in the Church. He keeps the Church going, keeps the Church moving forward. More and more, beyond the limits, onwards ... You cannot understand the Church of Jesus without this Paraclete, whom the Lord sends us for this very reason. He makes unthinkable choices, unimaginable! **Pope Francis**

Already in the New Testament, we experience two spiritual realities that are internally connected, which complement each other, but which are conveyed separately. Perhaps we can put it this way: Baptism is more of a Jesus sacrament. It unites us so profoundly with the Risen Lord that we are "one body" with him and with other Christians (something we celebrate in the Eucharist). Confirmation is more a a Spirit sacrament. In Confirmation, we are endowed with the Holy Spirit – who is also the Spirit of Jesus.

Question 59:
Why did God make human beings?

> So get rid of your old self, which made you live as you used to ... Your hearts and minds must be made completely new, and you must put on the new self, which is created in God's likeness and reveals itself in the true life that is upright and holy
>
> **Eph 4:22-24 (Good News Translation)**

In Confirmation, we become *spiritual* people. God himself dwells in the depths of our soul. From now on, we live from a source deeper than our deepest thoughts. We experience a drive within us that is greater than any willpower. God lives, loves and breathes in us. And so we no longer belong to Jesus just outwardly because we like him, or because we are his fans or because we agree with his teachings.

No, as spiritual people – as people who live from the Spirit – we are in a real "relationship" with Him. We are his.

Bishop Stefan Oster once said in a confirmation homily: "Belonging to him doesn't just mean we hang onto his dog collar and he's dragging us behind him. To belong to him is to be friends with him. We are children of God. We belong to him because we freely chose him." And later he told the confirmands: "Become relationship specialists for the relationship with God and help others find that relationship. We should be relationship specialists for our relationship with God, because we are learning better and better how to live in relationship with God, how this relationship grows, how we ourselves grow in it, how we ourselves are sustained by it. And we should help to bring other people with us into this relationship."

Y **Question 286:** What is freedom and what is it for?

Y **Question 340:** How is God's grace related to our freedom?

" To the degree one loves the Church, one has the Holy Spirit

St Augustine (354–430)

How does God reconcile us with himself and with others?

This unit talks about

why even the Pope
goes to confession
and why we cannot be a Christian
if we only ever settle matters
on our own.

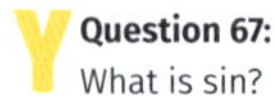

Question 67: What is sin?

Question 315: What is a sin in the first place?

It seems we live in the age of universal excuses. Whatever happens – it was our parents, the circumstances, politics or our neighbour. We like to deal with sin and guilt, but only when it concerns others.

1 Cor 15:3

Psychologists rightly point out that we cannot build a strong personality if we are constantly tearing ourselves apart and are thus unable to accept ourselves and feel good about ourselves. These days we know how important it is to give children recognition right from the start. But does that also mean excluding the subject of sin? After all, the New Testament says that Christ "died for our sins" (1 Cor 15:3). Crucifixes are still worn as pendants or found adorning rooms here and there. Is this just a relic from a dark past?

The taking leave of sin began in the 19th century. **Friedrich Nietzsche**, the radical philosopher, had something against "sin". He thought it was a "Jewish feeling and a Jewish invention" that made people sick – typical of a "religion of slaves". Sin was used to create "contrition, debasement, grovelling" and to humiliate people. "Only if you repent will God be merciful to you" had never occurred to a "healthy Greek." Nietzsche recommended "a carefree attitude to the natural consequences of sin." He dreamed of the vital beauty and power of the "fair-haired beast" without a conscience: "the beast must out again, must return to the wild – Roman, Arabian, Germanic, Japanese nobility, Homeric heroes, Scandinavian Vikings – in this requirement they are all alike."

Question 290: How does God help us to be free?

What the Nazis made of this is well known. Sin existed in National Socialism only as "sin against blood and race."

National ideologues saw to it that people lost their conscience and became blind to all the real factors of dehumanisation. Soon, there were blond "supermen" on the ramp, smiling devilishly as "subhumans" were loaded into cattle cars for transport to the gas chambers. This much should be clear: to gut the contents of sin, be casual about it, make it ridiculous, exclude it from human existence is a lie, and often enough a lifelong lie. "If we say that we have no sin, we deceive ourselves, and there is no truth in us" (1 John 1:8). The consequences are dramatic. A lie was / is, incidentally, the *original sin*, as can be read in Genesis. The Gospel of John speaks of "the father of all lies" (John 8:44) and considers him to be "from the very beginning the murderer" (John 8:44). This is the devil. There is no reason to trivialise him and play the "little devil".

Question 297: Can people form their conscience?

Question 312: How do we know that we have sinned?

Gen 1

Jn 8:44

The greatest trick the devil ever pulled was convincing the world he didn't exist.

Charles Baudelaire (1821–1867)

Question 453: What does our relationship with truth have to do with God?

Many people will go along with you this far. But they do not understand what sin has to do with God. Let's use a little device to help us. Let's replace the word "God" with the word "The Absolute" – and add a few more qualities: absolute beauty, absolute truth, absolute good. God cannot be defined, but insofar as he is beyond everything that is good, true, and beautiful in the world, everything that is not good, not true, and not beautiful looks somehow *absolutely impossible* when put beside God. Now, we human beings are always inclined to compromise. Imagine if there was a world in which Harvey Weinstein could, in the last instance, say: "I think that's really beautiful!", or where Donald Trump could ultimately say: "But I like it!", And Adani could end up saying : "But we think it's good!"

There should not be anyone in the world who has sinned, however much they may have possibly sinned, who, after they have looked into your eyes, would go away without having received your mercy, if they are looking for mercy.

Francis of Assisi (ca. 1181–1226)

Question 232: What must I bring to a confession?

However, there's God. He really is not distant from us. He is so close to us that everything that goes wrong here in our human world affects him *absolutely* – indeed, he feels it so deeply in his heart that he gives everything, even his own Son, to fix the world, to restore the good, the true, the beautiful and reconcile us with him and with each other. But God is not only to be found among the victims of sin when they are loaded into the wagons heading for Auschwitz. God also has a solution for the sinners. For small, medium and great sinners, and even for the Nazis-in-jackboots kind who wreak much greater havoc than they could ever be

> God is greater than our guilt.
>
> **Pope Francis**

able to redress. It is God himself who has reconciled us with himself through Jesus Christ, "making peace through the blood of his cross" (Col 1:20).

Col 1:20

Question 150: Can the Church really forgive sins?

We *would have to* pay, but he pays. Only one thing is required of us: to confess our sins. "In him we have redemption through his blood, the forgiveness of our trespasses" (Eph 1:7)

Eph 1:7

> That we "receive forgiveness of sins in his name" is the declaration of belief the apostles demanded as a baptismal confession. If this forgiveness had been proclaimed by Jesus only as a general truth, it would have nothing to do with the confession of his name. Once we've learned the lesson we can forget the teacher. Jesus, like Socrates, might say: Do not worry about Jesus, worry about the truth. But the Apostle writes, "In Him we have the forgiveness of our trespasses."

Robert Spaemann (1927–2019), German philosopher

Why is the Holy Mass the Church's central event?

THIS UNIT TALKS ABOUT

the astonishing observation that Catholic Christians believe a piece of bread is Jesus Christ. The question is, why?

Question 219: How often must a Catholic Christian participate in the celebration of the Eucharist?

When you ask someone on the street what is typical for Catholics, you hear, “They have to go to church every Sunday.” Well, that matter of “having to” do something can be a bit tricky. Does someone have to kiss his wife? Does he have to? Well, not really. But what value is love that doesn’t show itself in tenderness? Of similar importance is the question: Where is your Christianity if you do not go to where

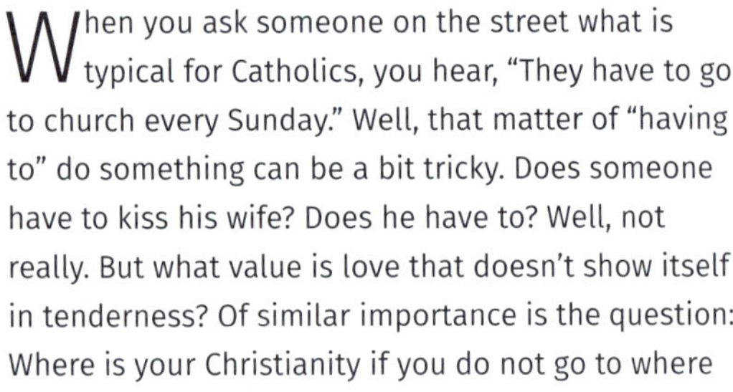

Jesus wants to meet with you? A modern response could be “My Christianity is where I want it to be.” But is it really the case that we can decide on all the crucial things in our life just by ourselves? We don’t decide whether we exist or not, when we are born or who our parents are. God does not follow our commands. Neither does he just turn up in the forest whenever we feel like seeing him. If you want to meet Jesus you are well advised to adapt to the places, signs and times that he has opened up for us.

Question 168: Why does the liturgy have priority in the life of the Church and of the individual?

But what does Jesus have to do with this incomprehensible Sunday event in a cold church? This needs to be explained. And we have to admit: what is actually happening could sometimes be made clearer. Where do we start? Maybe with the fact that the Holy Mass is not just one kind of worship among others, just a bit more solemn, so that one might choose from a range of offerings.

The Holy Mass has no rival. It is unique and it is not a matter of taste whether I would prefer Holy Mass or meditation in the crypt. To sum up its USP:
In the Holy Mass, you receive the body of Christ and, by consuming it, you become the "body of Christ" yourself. "Body of Christ" is just another name for church. Therefore nobody can say: I want to belong to the Church, but I don't want to be absorbed into it. That would be absurd.

Question 126: What does it mean to say that the Church is "the Body of Christ"?

USP
Unique Selling Point

But isn't it a bit like a passion play based on some past event, like the Passion Play Festival at Oberammergau in Bavaria? No, despite the amount of fake blood shed there, nobody dies. In the Holy Mass, Christ's sacrifice on the cross takes place anew for us. The priest is not staging an edifying performance of "The Last Supper". It actually takes place and we take part in it. It is not just some kind of mental exercise. It is real.

Question 216: In what way is Christ there when the Eucharist is celebrated?

preferred to the work of God. **St Benedict of Nursia** (ca. 480–547)

Now is the time for us to take a look at some of the most amazing things. Let's take a pan-shot with the camera in the Upper Room: this is the night when Jesus will be handed over – it is the eve of the (Jewish) Pasch. Jesus is doing what any Jewish head of the family would have done that night. He gathers his own around him – in this case the "Twelve" – to celebrate a kind of sacrificial liturgy, the "Eucharist" (= thanksgiving).

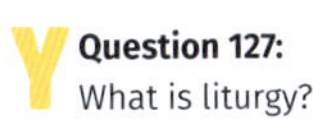

Question 127: What is liturgy?

Lk 22:19

Lk 22:20

Question 99: What happened at the Last Supper?

1 Cor 11:24

Lk 22:18

But in doing so, Jesus chooses some mysterious words that would have made the Apostles' blood curdle. He prays and makes an offering by taking up the bread and saying these words over it: "*This is my body* which is given for you" (Lk 22:19). Excuse me? He is sacrificing *himself*? What if a high priest had gotten wind of that! But it gets even worse. Jesus takes the goblet of wine and says, "'This cup that is poured out for you is the new covenant *in my blood*" (Lk 22:20). Imagine that: the covenant between the Twelve Tribes of Israel and God was the most sacred of things, and here is Jesus founding a New Covenant with another twelve in number, a bunch of common fisherman – and he founds this covenant on his blood. And the Apostles are supposed to eat and drink him in order to be accepted into this covenant. That is high treason! What is their Master doing! "Do this in remembrance of me" (1 Cor 11:24). What for? And what does that mean? "for I tell you that from now on I will not drink of the fruit of the vine until the kingdom of God comes" (Lk 22:18). I can imagine that someone like Judas thought to himself: this man is off his rocker!

It must be said that the Apostles had *no way of understanding* what Jesus was saying. Only after the bloody day on Golgotha, after the empty grave, after the encounters with the Risen One who broke the bread with them, would they know what Jesus meant by giving up his body, shedding his blood for us, the New Covenant, and thus the beginning of a new history of God with humankind, starting with Jesus. It is deeply moving to see how even the early Christians gathered on Sunday to celebrate this meal liturgy and to live from Jesus who distributed himself among them this way. The Church still springs from the Eucharist. So, please go to it.

Question 208: What is Holy Eucharist?

Question 220: What sort of preparation do I need in order to be able to receive Holy Eucharist?

3:44 Why is Mass so boring?

Those who go to communion lose themselves in God like a drop of water in the ocean. They can no more be separated. When we have just gone to communion, if we were asked, "What are you taking home?" we might answer, "I am carrying Heaven home." A saint said that we were Christ-bearers. It is very true; but we do not have enough faith. We do not comprehend our dignity. When we leave the holy banquet we are as happy as the Wise Men would have been if they could have carried the Infant Jesus away with them.

St Jean Marie Vianney (1786–1859), Curé of Ars

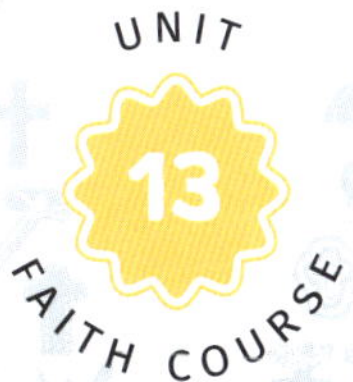

How does God call us?

This unit talks about

optimising our life story.

Christians do not plan their lives

on a drawing board,

but by listening to God.

What does God want from me?

What am I here for?

Question 18: What significance does the New Testament have for Christians?

Question 8: How does God reveal himself in the Old Testament?

In ancient religions, the "gods" were mostly silent, fickle figures. If the weather was not right, the harvest failed and war plans failed, then you knew that the gods were angry. You had to beseech them a bit more, sacrifice a bit more, then the world would be right again. Even among Christians you can still find remnants of this primitive image of God.

Gen 12:2

The fact that God is different, quite different from what people like to imagine, dawned on humanity a few thousand years ago in the Middle East. Abraham suddenly encounters a God within reach, a God who *wants* something ... and not burnt offerings, animal or even human sacrifice: "Go from your country and your kindred and your father's house to the land that I will show you!"(Gen 12:1). What God wants is completely in the interests of this nomadic prince. "You will be a blessing" (Gen 12:2) With Abraham begins the endless story of a God who intervenes: blessing, *summoning and calling*, more and more clearly *calling people out of hardship*. A few people experience that, eventually the people of Israel, and finally the whole world. This becomes fully clear with Jesus Christ who not only calls fishermen to fish for people (Mk 1:17) – i.e. a special ministry – but also has a calling in mind for each individual human being: He "desires everyone to be saved and to come to the knowledge of the truth" (1 Tim 2:4)

Mk 1:17

1 Tim 2:4

Jesus' fundamental concern is to bring people into a relationship of communication, love and friendship with God. And he gets himself involved in a divine way: "Come to *me*, all you that are weary and are carrying heavy burdens!" (Mt 11:28)

Mt 11:28

Mother Teresa (1910–1997) gave serious thought to *vocation, God who calls us*: "You are special to God. He wants to honour you by filling you with his presence. He called you, you belong to him. When you realise this, you can get through every mistake, every humiliation, every suffering – when you recognise the personal love of Jesus for you and yours for him."

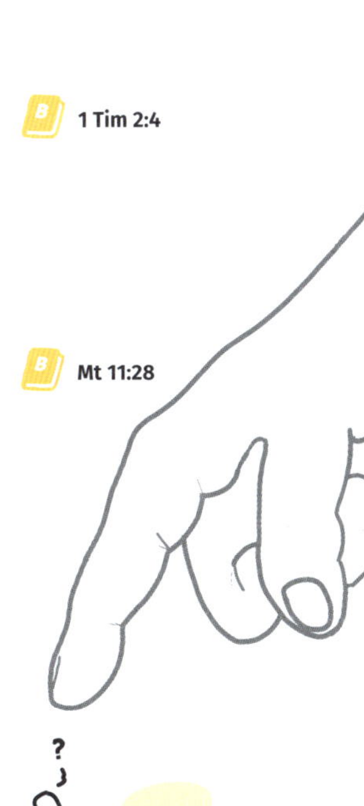

By the way, every calling is unique. Often it is not we who have chosen what God calls us to and where he places us. I know a woman who is called to be with one dying person after another, because she is so good at helping people pass to their Eternal home. Today she knows: "This is my vocation!"

> If a man is called to be a street sweeper, he should sweep streets even as a Michaelangelo painted, or Beethoven composed music or Shakespeare wrote poetry. He should sweep streets so well that all the hosts of heaven and earth will pause to say, 'Here lived a great street sweeper who did his job well.'

Martin Luther King (1929–1968)

Now, there are not just general vocations in the church. What is the special vocation of a bishop or a priest? The shortest answer is: he is a successor of the Apostles. He does what the Apostles did. In the New Testament we find a kind of original Church structure. Jesus Christ is the Lord of the Church for all time.
He is the main character. He forgives sins. He teaches. He heals. He sacrifices himself. Around Jesus are his disciples. Jesus brought them close to him and into a kind of school. They watch Jesus from close up, talk to him. They take up his intentions. They are sent out to two by two "to every town and place where he himself intended to go" (Luke 10:1). Jesus no longer calls these disciples "servants" but "friends" (John 15:15). The disciples are the driving force of the Church and it may be the key to the Church crisis in our time that there is a lack of disciples and discipleship – people who are committed to Jesus' mission in their normal surrounds out of a personal relationship with Christ. We might think of Religious when it comes to *disciples*, but they are only living emblematically what *all disciples* should be doing.

Question 1: For what purpose are we here on earth?

Question 342: Are we all supposed to become saints?

Question 137: Why is the Church called apostolic?

Question 11: Why do we hand on the faith?

Jesus now takes some from among the disciples – the Apostles; he directs them towards the Church and an irreplaceable service within it, we could say. They do by proxy what only Jesus can do, building up the Church through the sacraments, in particular breaking bread (1 Cor 11:23,24) and forgiving sins: "If you forgive the sins of any, they are forgiven them" (Jn 20:23), but they also proclaim the message "whether the time is favourable or unfavourable" and guide people in Jesus' name. The public often question the role of priests today, not only because of celibacy. Some believe that a church can be organised quite well without priests, but that is wrong. While we can

Question 139: What is the lay vocation?

1 Cor 11: 23

Jn 20:23

> The priest is a monstrance whose obligation is to show Jesus. The priest must disappear so that others can see only Jesus

Charles de Foucauld (1858–1916)

discuss celibacy, because it is a “highly appropriate” sign required by the Church – after all, the celibate form of life was how Jesus lived – a Church without priests is unthinkable; it would destroy its inner matrix. By the way: where a church produces disciples, vocations to the priesthood also come about.

Question 259: How is the universal priesthood of all the faithful different from the ordained priesthood?

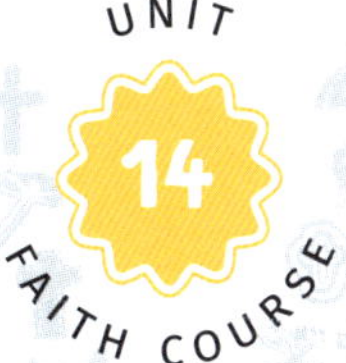

What does it mean to live a celibate life in the Church?

THIS UNIT TALKS ABOUT

why Don Camillo was
full of love and by no means lonely.
In real life, too, priests are
people of relationship:
they live from God.

Question 265: Are all people called to marriage?

 **Mt 19:12**

I am always surprised when lay people have no greater problem with the Church than "celibacy". No one forces Christians to follow Jesus' counsel, namely, to live unmarried "for the sake of the kingdom of heaven" (Mt 19:12). After all, no Christian has to live that way. Unfortunately, some religious and priests are bad advocates for celibacy. Once, at a Catholic Convention, I witnessed a strange debate. The head of a seminary put forward the thesis that celibacy should make the candidates happy – indeed, that they have to choose this way of life (with all its emotional deprivations), because no other form of life feels right for them. Another priest told him angrily that this was outrageous: what normal person would enjoy that? The man with the daring thesis stuck to his view. The whole thing, of course, was counterproductive.

Question 145: Why does Jesus want there to be Christians who live their whole life in poverty, unmarried chastity and obedience?

First of all it's fair to say: it's immediately obvious why religious live an unmarried life. With regard to priests, Uniate Catholic Churches have had married priests from time immemorial. The Roman Catholic Church has demanded celibacy from its bishops and priests for about a thousand years – and could change that. But there would have to be very good reasons to do so. First of all, though, we have to realise that there weren't just spiritual but also political reasons for enforcing priestly celibacy. If blood ties are involved

A great problem for Christianity in the world today is that no one thinks of the future with God: this world seems sufficient. We want only this world, to live only in this world. So we close the door to the true greatness of our existence. The meaning of celibacy as an anticipation of the future opens these doors, making the world greater, showing the reality of the future that seems to us already present.

Pope Benedict XVI.

> Celibacy goes deeper than the flesh

F. Scott Fitzgerald American fiction writer (1896–1940)

in the priesthood then it means that there is a great risk of the sacred becoming an heirloom and family property.

But let us quickly list the reasons against celibacy. First of all there is the problem that some people obviously choose this way of life without inner conviction. Secondly, there is the scandal of abuse, which gives many outsiders the impression that clerics are sexually over-charged without exception, which is in no way the case. But suddenly in public opinion this wonderful symbol of the existence of another world has become a disastrous counter-symbol, especially as it is often boys who have been abused by priests. Apparently, a not insignificant number of men without a vocation and with immature sexual development have felt drawn to this ministry. Hopefully, those responsible have realised this. Thirdly, there is the lack of priests, which is also due to the high entry bar that

Y **Question 386:** Why does the Fifth Commandment protect the physical and spiritual integrity of a human being as well?

is celibacy. Linked to this are the increasing number of congregations where the Eucharist can no longer be celebrated regularly because they don't have a priest any more. Some dioceses have almost no new arrivals to the priesthood at all.

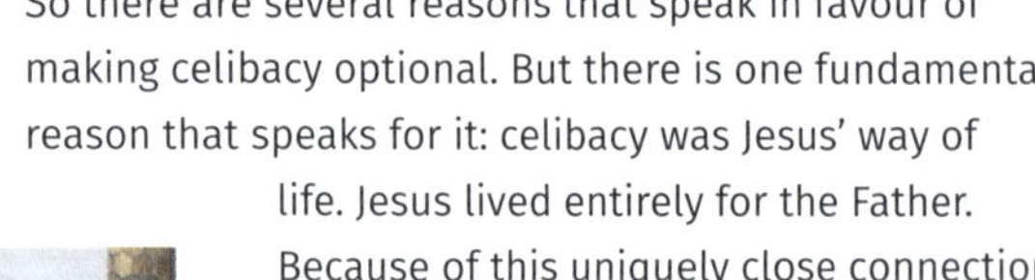

So there are several reasons that speak in favour of making celibacy optional. But there is one fundamental reason that speaks for it: celibacy was Jesus' way of life. Jesus lived entirely for the Father. Because of this uniquely close connection with heaven Jesus was wholly there for the people. That he had a mistress by the name of Mary Magdalene on the side, was even married, is an invention of B-class writers. It was Jesus Himself who invited people into this provocative "all for God" way of life. And already in the early Church, the conviction arose that it is good for the successors of the Apostles – today bishops and priests – to also live like Jesus. In Jesus, the old worldly cycle of begetting, giving birth, dying breaks apart; "For the present form of this world is passing away" (1 Cor 7:31). Celibates, who have received this gift in their heart from God (Mt 19:11, "Not everyone can accept this teaching, but only those to whom it is given"), carry out this radical newness of the world to come that began with Jesus. God is already, now, "everything" that human beings need. One day we too will understand Teresa of Avila: "Whoever has God lacks nothing: God alone suffices."

Question 92: Why did Jesus call apostles?

1 Cor 7:31
Mt 19:11

Question 250: How does the Church understand the sacrament of Holy Orders?

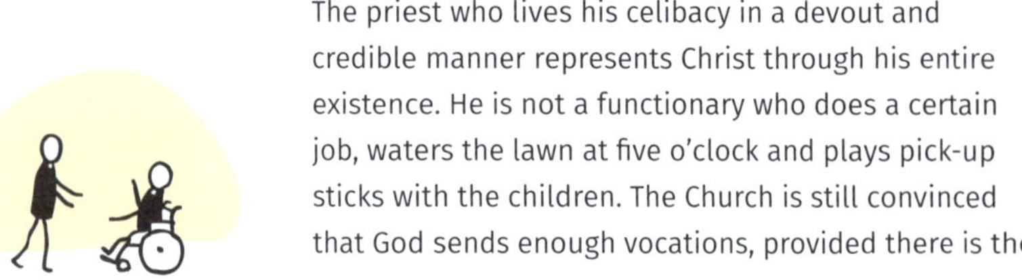

The priest who lives his celibacy in a devout and credible manner represents Christ through his entire existence. He is not a functionary who does a certain job, waters the lawn at five o'clock and plays pick-up sticks with the children. The Church is still convinced that God sends enough vocations, provided there is the

fertile ground of true discipleship and the following of Christ. That may be the reason why in some places there is an abundance of candidates for the priesthood while in others seminaries lament the lack of them and religious houses stand empty.

At any rate, presenting the priesthood as a conventional, normal career opportunity and a position for graduate theologians cannot be the solution. Incidentally, the word CELIBACY should be done away

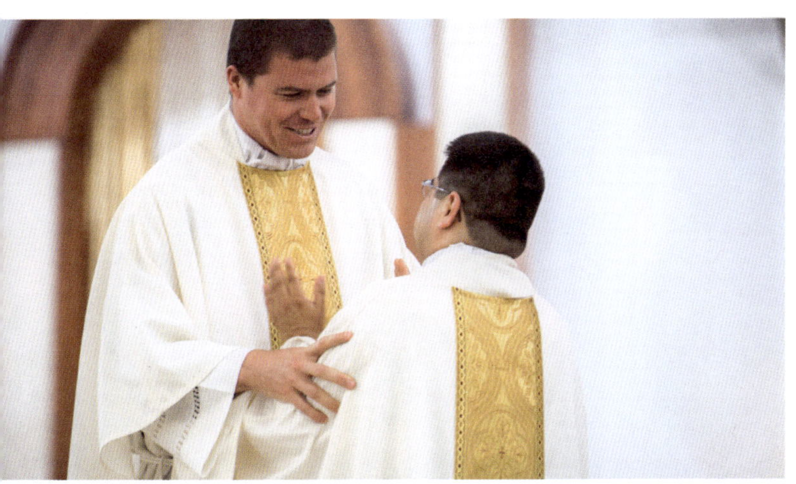

with. It misses the point. It comes from *caelebs* = unmarried (apparently). This is precisely what must not happen under any circumstances to the person who does not marry for the sake of the kingdom: that he lives for himself. Either he is "in relationship", namely in a love story with God that is capable of development, or he becomes an eccentric bachelor. The emblematically lived "celibacy" is something social: it is love, attachment, community. Therefore, the audacity of celibacy is closer to the resolve of marriage than to the way some single people are unable to form attachments.

CELIBACY

Y **Question 122:** Why does God want there to be a Church?

4.21: Why choose celibacy if people are made for marriage?

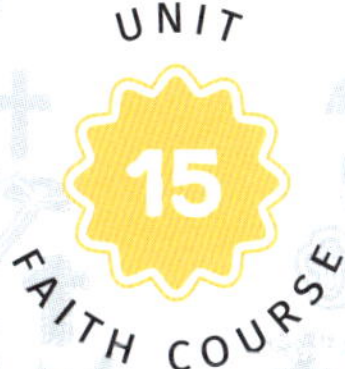

What does getting married mean in the Church?

This unit talks about

why it is
absolutely essential
to find the person who is worth
taking along to the church, before the altar,
and in other respects too.

Question 400: What does it mean to say that we are sexual beings?

Question 64: Why did God create us male and female?

Question 401: Is there a priority of one sex over another?

That God created human beings as *man and woman* is perhaps one of his best inventions. What kind of a sad world would it be if there was no love and eroticism and all the fascinating differences between men and women? 6500 genes work differently in men and women. Nevertheless, a woman who has to work in an all-women office might hear a sympathetic comment from another woman: "Only women, how can you stand it!" or a man might sympathise with a colleague who finds himself working only with other men: "Only men, how dull is that!" Not only did God create men and women differently – he also created them for each other, so that they complement each other and, together, offer us a glimpse of what God is like.

Most people are afraid that they will lose their freedom when they love, and cannot believe that love is simultaneously the greatest development of freedom.

Erich Fromm (1900–1980)

God seems to be well aware that men are from Mars and women from Venus; it is as if it were a trick of his that he has only made a single platform on which man and woman come together permanently: *love*. That the love between man and woman leads to marriage is not something invented by mothers-in-law; it is inherent to human nature and love itself that two people commit themselves to each other without reservation.

Question 402:
What is love?

Question 260:
Why did God dispose man and woman for each other?

Love is something very deep – a state in which this other person appears to be worth any price to the other, even their own life. Love makes you crazy enough to give yourself for good to someone else without any further conditions.

If I get sick? No matter! If I'm going to go grey someday? To me, you will never be ugly. Albert Camus said: "To love a person means to agree to grow old with them." Love is a gift. You do not take gifts back. A husband and wife create a space of warmth in which children can arrive and grow up happy.

> To love someone is to see a miracle invisible to others.
>
> **Francois Mauriac** (1885–1970)

Question 418: What is the significance of the child in a marriage?

Question 261: How does the sacrament of Matrimony come about?

However, Pope Francis says: “Marriage is a work of every day, I could say a craft work, a goldsmith’s work, because the husband has the task to make his wife more woman and the wife has the task to make her husband more man. I am thinking of you that one day you will walk along the streets of your town and the people will say: ‘Look at that beautiful woman, so strong! ...’ ‘With the husband that she has, it’s understandable!’ And to you too: ‘Look at him and how he is! ...’ “With the wife he has, I can understand why!’ It’s this, reaching this point: making one another grow together, one another.”

” But my rose, all on her own, is more important than all of you together, since she’s the one I’ve watered ... Since she’s the one I listened to when she complained, or when she boasted, or even sometimes when she said nothing at all. Since she’s my rose.

Antoine de Saint-Exupéry (1900–1944)

For something that is risky to hold as true in a purely human sense, man and woman give themselves to one another before a priest in the "sacrament of matrimony". They give each other the sacrament. That's more than any marriage contract could accomplish. God offers a covenant to the couple; he brings himself into this union of a man and a woman and joins them in the depths of his own irrevocable divine love: "Therefore, what God has joined together, let no one separate" (Mt 19:6).

Before the two promise each other faithful love "until death do us part", it must be clear what belongs to marriage. This includes sex, which will surprise some people. After all, marriage does not come about only through a promise, but also through a husband and wife sleeping together and becoming "one flesh" (Mt 19:5). And people always think God does not care about sex!

Y **Question 424:** What is adultery? Is divorce the appropriate response?

B **Mt 19:6**

Y **Question 404:** What is chaste love? Why should a Christian live a chaste life?

When Jesus emphasises the indissolubility of marriage, he does not impose some commandment to shackle people; rather, he frees them to expect love not only from one another, but from him. Only with God are these words in the famous ode to love true: "Love never ceases" (1 Cor 13:8).

1 Cor 13:8

A broken marriage is a broken world

Gertrude Fussenegger (1912–2009), Austrian writer

And there are other conditions: the two must be free of ties when they step before the altar to be married; and their promise must be all-embracing and public. Both have to be ready to take this step of their own free will. If one of the two is acting under duress, fear, internal or external pressure at the time of marriage, the marriage will not be valid. You should not marry because mum or dad wants it, or because you finally want to get out of the house. You should not marry in the Church if you are thinking, secretly: "Why not give it a try! It'll last as long as it lasts!" Nor does the so-called marriage consent mean anything if one or both partners in the dream is not definitely ready to leave extramarital affairs aside. And there is one last hurdle left: Both must be open to having children. If one of them secretly thinks "Count me out!", then it is not a marriage.

Question 417: What significance does the sexual encounter have within marriage?

Question 262: What is necessary for a Christian, sacramental marriage?

Set me as a seal upon your heart,
as a seal upon your arm;
for love is strong as death,
passion fierce as the grave.
Its flashes are flashes of fire,
a raging flame

Song 8:6

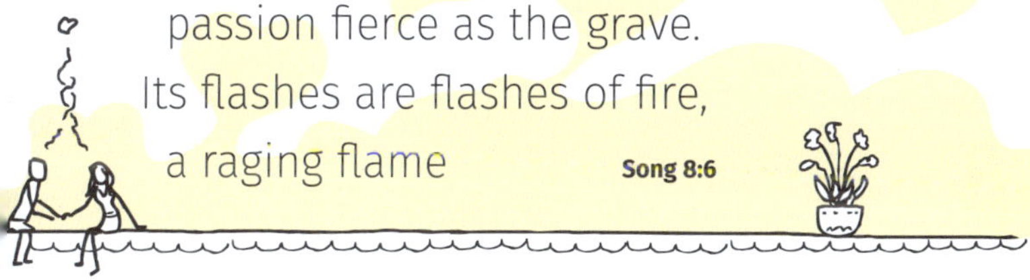

However, we will only discover the full beauty and greatness of Christian marriage if we understand it as a parable of God's faithfulness and devotion: "Husbands, love your wives, just as Christ loved the church and gave himself up for her ... Therefore husbands should love their wives as they do their own bodies" (Eph 5:25, 28a)

Eph 5:25

What do the Commandments have to do with love?

This unit talks about

how to act well and with love
and why there's a need
for some accompanying measures
so as not to be taken in by
our own stuff and nonsense.

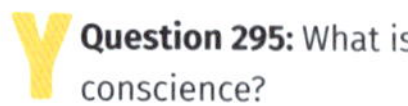

Question 295: What is conscience?

Question 298: Are the people who act wrongly in good conscience guilty in God's sight?

Conscience is a delicate thing. Not a few get through life without it, which led Stanislaw Lec to utter his most famous line: "His conscience was clean – he never used it!" Others do use their conscience; but they invoke it mostly when they are about to commit their worst deeds. Small-scale; it's what theatre thrives on, just like history on a larger scale. In the name of their personal conscience people lie, cheat, betray and commit adultery. There is no sin that hasn't been committed "with a clear conscience" and by bypassing the commandments.

Question 291: How can people tell whether their action is good or bad?

The Auxiliary Bishop of Cologne, Bishop Dick, once told a splendid story to explain how conscience and commandments relate to each other: Let's take the case of the children playing football in the living room. Dad comes in and is horrified.

> Conscience – there are two ways of regarding conscience; one as a mere sort of sense of propriety, a taste teaching us to do this or that, the other as the echo of God's voice. Now all depends on this distinction — the first way is not of faith, and the second is of faith

St John Henry Newman (1801–1890)

"Don't you realise that there is a very valuable old China vase here? If you smash it, Mum will be heartbroken! Please go outside with the ball!" The children now have the choice: either they go outside or they continue to kick it in the living room and risk the disaster. So, the children know "the commandment". Their conscience has been made more aware, because they now know about the bad consequences of a wrong decision. And this is how it always should feel when you invoke your conscience. You need to check your actions against the Commandments. And to do that, you need to know the Ten Commandments (cf. Ex 20:17 and Dt 5:6, 21). We need to know that lying, pride, robbery, envy, jealousy, slander, adultery and murder are never permissible, nor even advisable options for action.

Ex 20:17
Dt 5:6, 21

Now, some people see a contrast between Jesus who brought love, and the Old Testament, by which they mean a bad legalistic kind of religion. They quote St Augustine, who once said "love and (then) do what you want" and use the quotation to gloss over their sexual indiscretions. But neither Augustine nor Jesus can be misappropriated here. Augustine is to be understood as follows: if you really had recognised love and were acting out of love, you would not need the commandments, you would act perfectly. And, of course, in the oft-quoted (and seldom read) Sermon on the Mount, Jesus says, "For truly I tell you, until heaven and earth pass away, not one letter, not one stroke of a letter, will pass from the law until all is accomplished. Therefore, whoever breaks one of the least of these commandments, and teaches others to do the same, will be called least in the kingdom of heaven; but whoever does them and teaches them will be called great in the kingdom of heaven" (Mt 5:18, 19).

Y **Question 309:** What is charity (love)?

Y **Question 349:** What are the Ten Commandments?

Y **Question 351:** Aren't the Ten Commandments outmoded?

Mt 15:18-19

Jesus not only inculcates the commandments, he

even makes them more rigorous: “You have heard that it was said to those of ancient times, ‘You shall not murder’; and ‚whoever murders shall be liable to judgement.’ But I say to you that if you are angry with a brother or sister, you will be liable to judgement” (Mt 5:21, 22).

Mt 5:21–22

Question 348: “Teacher, what … must I do to have eternal life?” (Mt 19:16)

Mk 12:30

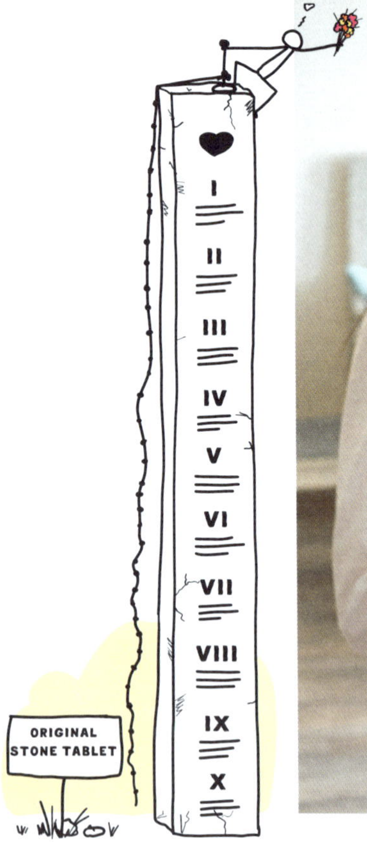

But it is the same Jesus who sums up the Commandments in the commandment of love. According to this, you must first love God “with all your heart, and with all your soul, and with all your mind, and with all your strength” (Mk 12:30). A close second is, you shall "love your neighbour as yourself. There is no other commandment greater than these" (Mk 12:31). But did not the Old Testament already call for love of God and neighbour? That's true. So what is new about it when Jesus says: "I give you a new commandment, that you love one another"(Jn 13:34)? The novelty of the new commandment of love is that Jesus makes himself the standard and benchmark of love: "Just as I have loved you, you also should love one another" (Jn 13:34) And what did Jesus do in terms of love, that makes him the standard? He died for us, as Paul says "while we were [God's] enemies" (Rom 5:10). In short, the new thing about the new commandment of love is *love of our enemy*: "You have heard that it was said, 'You shall love your neighbour and hate your enemy.' But I say to you, I Love your enemies and pray for those who persecute you"(Mt 5:43-44). À la Jesus. This love of one's enemies is something so unique in religious history that Muslim writer Navid Kermani once said that Christians had every reason to be proud of it and wear it like a precious circlet on their foreheads.

Mk 12:30-31

Question 337: How are we saved?

Jn 13:34

Question 34: What should you do once you have come to know God?

Rom 5:10

Mt 5:43-44

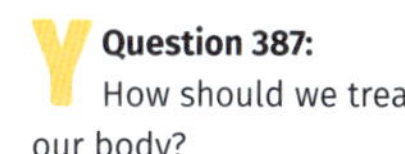
Question 387: How should we treat our body?

Even if our heart does not have love, it still has a longing for love, and thus the beginnings of love.

St Francis de Sales (1567–1622)

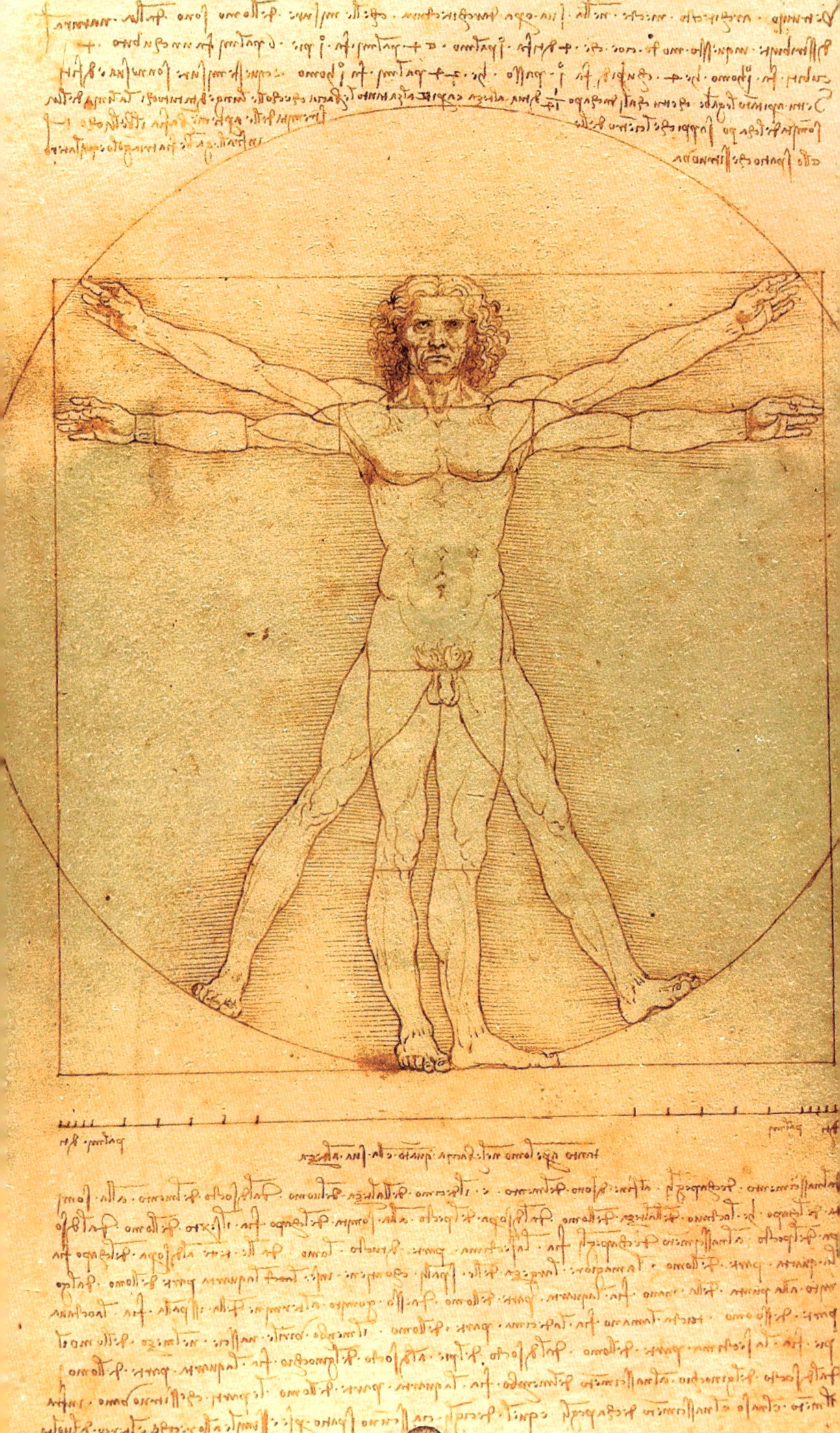

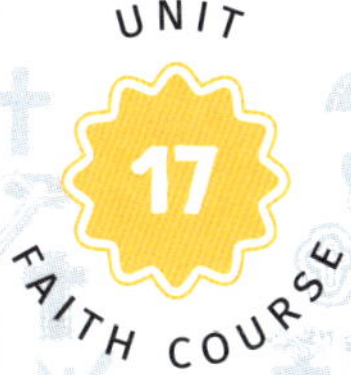

What makes a human being human?

This unit talks about

a somewhat embarrassing incident
with a naked emperor
and the question as to what
a human being
is worth and
how to get body,
mind and soul
into top
condition.

Question 301: How does a person become prudent?

Question 303: What does it mean to have fortitude?

Among folk tales, there is one about a vain Emperor who cared for nothing but his clothes. One day he came across two swindlers pretending to be able to weave the finest fabrics. The Emperor's new clothes would be so fine that they could only be seen by wise and worthy persons. The two pretended to weave some clothing, and finally gave the emperor clothes that in truth consisted of nothing but air. The Emperor could easily see in front of the mirror that he was naked, but his vanity did not allow him to admit he was a fool. The chamberlains and ministers were enthusiastic as well. They bowed with exclamations of admiration. So the Emperor stepped out onto the street. And the same thing kept happening: no one wanted to compromise themselves; everyone admired the Emperor's new clothes. Only one child exclaimed: "The Emperor is naked!" ...

Question 300: Why do we have to work to form our character?

Question 163: What is the Last Judgement?

No one likes to be naked. Therefore, we not only surround ourselves with clothes, but also with titles, merits, qualifications, salaries, classy cars and lots of "friends" on Facebook. We invent glamorous biographies that we ourselves ultimately believe in. But appearances can fit badly. Crises and illnesses, culpable failure and simple bad luck make the facade crumble. When St Francis was about to die, he asked to be placed naked on the floor of the Portiuncula. Did not the biblical Job say: "Naked I came from my mother's womb, and naked shall I return there"(Job 1:21)? And were not Luther's final words: "We are beggars, this is true!" Yes, it's true. When we ultimately appear before the Lord, we are naked. It no longer matters what we were in the world, how many companies we founded, how many houses we built. More likely we will be asked if we were

clothed in “compassion, kindness, humility, meekness, and patience” (Col 3:12). We will be asked if we were “human”.

 **Col 3:12**

> All human beings are born free and equal in dignity and rights.

United Nations Universal Declaration of Human Rights

But what makes a human being actually human? Spontaneously, we have a very noble notion of what a human being is – but we only need a single instance of conflict with it and this noble idea bursts like a soap bubble. Is a child in the womb *human, half human, not human*? And the old, demented woman in the nursing home – is she still human or already a meaningless remnant being whose disposal one should be thinking about? Is a board member at Mercedes worth more than an orphan boy in Mumbai? Christians wisely do not get into such discussions. For them, the human being's worth is not up for discussion, cannot be measured. Human beings have an enduring, unique dignity. This dignity is not grounded in the person's humanness but in God the Creator, Sustainer, Redeemer and Judge. The dignity of every human being results from his or her relationship with God. God has looked upon this

Question 382: Is it permissible to offer assistance in dying?

Question 383: Why is abortion unacceptable at any phase in the development of an embryo?

4.27: What is wrong with prenatal testing?

> Everything has either a price or a dignity. Whatever has a price can be replaced by something else as its equivalent; on the other hand, whatever is above all price, and therefore admits of no equivalent, has a dignity

Immanuel Kant (1724–1804), German philosopher

Is 43:1

PS 17:8

Mt 25

person in love and never looks away again: "I have called you by name, you are mine" (Is 43:1). We belong, so to speak, to royalty, we are untouchable. Therefore, because they are the "apple" of God's eye (Ps 17:8), we must not classify people, not exploit them. And because the poorest of the poor are always the first victims, Matthew recounts the most astonishing parable in all of Scripture. It could be called *the parable of God's solidarity*. They are all listed in Chapter 25: the hungry, the thirsty, the strangers, the naked, the sick, prisoners. The key is in verse 40: "Truly I tell you, just as you did it to one of the least of these who are members of my family, you did it to me." Me! Jesus makes himself one of the poor. In the poor you are touching him!

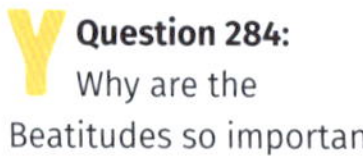
Question 284: Why are the Beatitudes so important?

This is incomprehensible – as incomprehensible as the beatitudes, the heart of the Sermon on the Mount. Here, nobody is singing the praises of the successful, the rich, the stars, the VIPs, the powerful and sovereigns. In the kingdom of God it is *the others* who are blessed – the poor, those who mourn, the meek, the hungry, the persecuted and all who stand

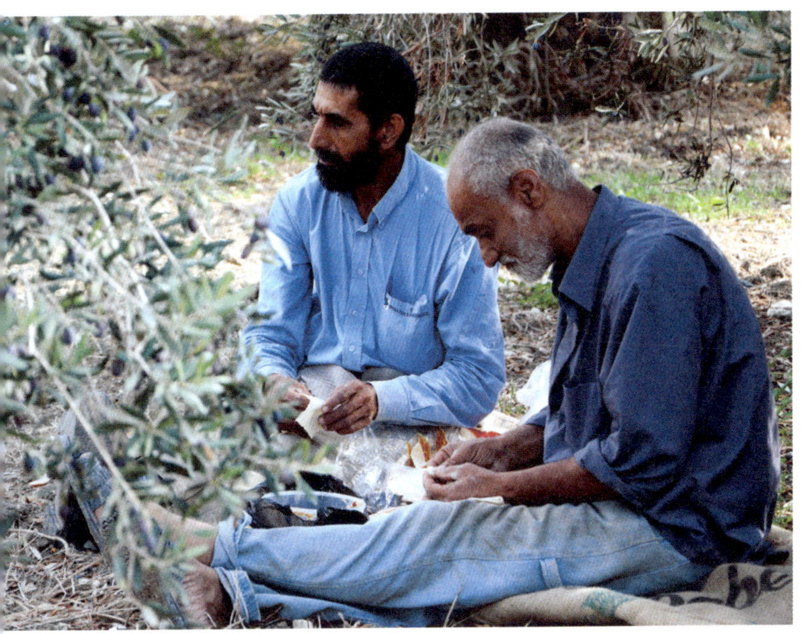

by their side: those who fight for justice, the merciful, people with a pure heart, the peacemakers. The world becomes humane through "mercy". St John Paul II has reminded us of this and Pope Francis no less. But it was already the Saint of Assisi who pinpointed the essence of being Christian: "There should not be anyone in the world who has sinned, however much they may have possibly sinned, who, after they have looked into your eyes, would go away without having received your mercy, if they are looking for mercy."

Question 89: To whom does Jesus promise "the kingdom of God"?

Question 329: How does social justice come about in a society?

Man is connected with all living things through his earthly origins, but is only human because God "breathed" a soul into him. That gives him his unmistakable dignity, but also his unique responsibility.

Christoph Cardinal Schönborn

TRALCO
TRALCO

What sets me free? What restricts me?

THIS UNIT TALKS ABOUT

aviation, aircraft and other
fast means of transport
that give you a sense of freedom.
But it is also about
the purpose of freedom
and why it could be the
opposite of freedom
to exercise every possible
freedom.

"Above the clouds," songwriter **Reinhard Mey** sang, "Freedom must be limitless." The song is about someone watching from the hangar as a plane takes off into the sky; he is overwhelmed by yearning and the wistful thought as to whether this freedom exists somewhere in which "all fears, all worries" remain behind or at least diminish. Reinhard Mey has lived this dream of every human being intensely. From 1972 he gradually gained his pilot's licence for single-engined and twin-engined aircraft, biplanes and helicopters, then for aerobatics and instrument flights, plus boat licences and a motorcycle licence. Reinhard Mey's biography reads like a sequence of moments of freedom. But Mey not only used his freedom to create ever new individual experiences of freedom; he also used his freedom to become active in social issues in an impressive way.

Y **Question 286:** What is freedom and what is it for?

Y **Question 289:** Must we allow people to use their free will, even when they decide in favour of evil?

4.2: What should I do with my life?

What is freedom? Freedom - and the desire for freedom - is something deeply human. That is how God made us, with a taste for freedom, for thinking things over, making choices, casually creating something. In freedom a human being is proud, dignified, beautiful. Freedom means to act completely of one's own accord, to create a piece of the world as we would like it to be, and not be determined by others. That is an important point, also in the Church. As much as parents would like their children to believe, it is just as wrong to persuade them to believe or to put pressure on them. God wants every person's freely given "yes". Anywhere that someone does not act completely of their own accord, where they are forced or pushed, they aren't fully human.

How free is the human being? The first answer is that human beings are free to do or not do whatever they want, even if it is objectively wrong. This is part of their human dignity, even if time and time again the powers that be try to curtail people in their civil liberties (freedom of religion, opinion, profession, assembly and association, etc.) because they think they know better what is good for people.

Question 354: Can people be forced to believe in God?

> Commandments are by no means arbitrarily imposed duties ... They protect man from the destructive power of egoism, hatred, and hypocrisy. They show him all the false gods that make him a slave: self-love that excludes God, lust for power and desire for pleasure which overthrow the legal order and demean our human dignity and that of our neighbour.

St John Paul II (1920–2005)

However, this praise of freedom should not overlook the fact that the option to choose evil – meaning things that damage themselves and others – can lead human beings straight onto the "highway to hell". It was occultist Aleister Crowley who issued the supposed freedom slogan: "Do what thou wilt shall be the whole of the Law!" This concept of freedom, which includes self-destruction and destruction of others (for example abortion, euthanasia, suicide) is based on a blasphemous substitution of God: *I* am the Lord; *I* am the law. No one else in the universe is

Question 287: But doesn't "freedom" consist of being able to do evil as well?

Question 49: Does God guide the world and my life?

really interested in what happens to me. Neither is there anyone who cares if others end up victims of my freedom.

The true God gives us full freedom. But he has built an orientation into freedom, an inner tendency towards what is good. I am entirely free, but the purpose of my freedom is what is good. Human beings are free so they can do good of their own free choice. This is why people feel a natural satisfaction when they do something good, and they blush with shame when caught doing wrong. That there is this distinction at all is an indication that good comes from the one who is good, or in other words: that the ultimate reason is that God is good. If God is good, then good is good and evil is simply evil. In a meaningful world, God wants us to be good. CS Lewis: "If we do not want to be what God wants us to be, then we really want something that cannot possibly make us happy."

Question 281: Why do we yearn for happiness?

Question 59: Why did God make human beings?

Incidentally, Reinhard Mey has personally experienced the limits of freedom. Two of his flight instructors crashed and died. One of his children died after being in a vegetative state for five years which – according to Reinhard Mey – "shook the family to its core and turned life upside down from one day to the next." Mey had spent countless nights at this son's bedside (his son was 32 when he died), singing songs, talking to him. Did he sing "Above the Clouds" to him? We probably need to talk about the human dream of freedom based on the premise that perfect freedom

Question 340: How is God's grace related to our freedom?

exists only where "all fears, all worries" have disappeared because there is one of whom it is said, "He will wipe every tear from their eyes: death will be no more; mourning and crying and pain will be no more." (Rev 21:4). Until then we should just be good, even if it is hard work.

Rev 21:4

> We impose our faith on no one.
> Such proselytism is contrary to Christianity.
> Faith can develop only in freedom.
> But we do appeal to the freedom of men
> and women to open their hearts to God,
> to seek him, to hear his voice.

Pope Benedict XVI

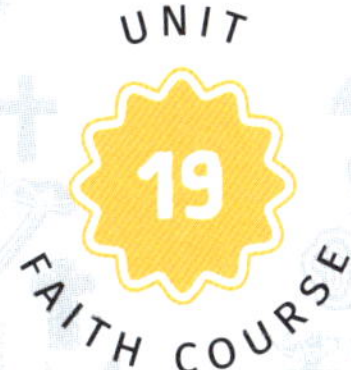

What does "Keep holy the Sabbath Day" mean?

THIS UNIT TALKS ABOUT

some very good reasons
for doing nothing.
God appreciates our work
but it is not the be-all and end-all.
God himself rested on the seventh day
and he wants our week to flow into
the joy of celebration.

Mothers know the situation: "What did you do with my Royal Doulton china teapot?" – "But ... it had a chip in it!" Drama. Revolt. Tears. Mum has laid a finger on a sacred item. The most ordinary things can be "sacred" to adults as well: an old pipe, a scratched vinyl record collection, whatever. In any case, it's not about the material value of a thing. The teapot, the deceased father's pipe, the Bob Dylan record – they stand for something greater, to which I feel attached via a symbol. Sunday is currently dying. And few are shedding a tear over this symbol.

Y **Question 187:** How important is Sunday?

" We can see in the history of the last century that in the States where God→

And yet, the request to make Sundays "holy" is not just a nice tip from the "Home & Gardens" magazine, but a divine command – number three of the Ten Commandments. Throughout the Old Testament there is scarcely a more dramatic staging than the scene in which Moses receives the "Ten Commandments" from God and comes down from the mountain with the tablets of the law for his people: "all the people witnessed the thunder and lightning, the sound of the trumpet, and the mountain smoking" (Ex 20:18). Why does God spend so much time and effort on how we organise our /leisure activities?

At the beginning of the Bible stands a God who makes it clear for all time that work is not everything and not even paramount. In the book of Genesis, the Creator himself indulges in a kind of pleasurable break: "So God blessed the seventh day and hallowed it, because on it God rested from all the work that he had done in creation" (Gen 2: 3). The people of Israel did as God did: they rested. Israel thought back to its time of slavery in Egypt and extended this sacred pause even to slaves, the cattle, donkeys, resident foreigners in the towns (Dt 5:14).

Y **Question 47:** Why did God rest on the seventh day?

was abolished, not only was the economy destroyed, but above all the souls **Pope Benedict XVI**

For Israel, the Sabbath was important because God was so important: he was the cause of everything, why everything had life; he was their Liberator, their Saviour. That had to be remembered – and yet it fell by the wayside in the course of everyday life. They needed something bigger (or, a clear sign) to remind them of God. The Sabbath day celebration evoked the presence of God at weekly intervals, made it palpable, filled them with unprecedented hope. "If Israel were to truly keep the Sabbath just once," the Talmud says, "the Messiah would come, for keeping the Sabbath is equal to keeping all the commandments."

Y **Question 362:** Why do Jews celebrate the Sabbath?

> This is the day that the Lord has made; let us rejoice and be glad in it.

Ps 118:24

Question 363: How does Jesus deal with the Sabbath?

Question 364: Why do Christians replace the Sabbath with Sunday?

This is the point where Old Testament and New Testament, Judaism and Christianity, Sabbath and Sunday separate. The Jews are still waiting for the Messiah; the Christians believe he came, and refer to Jesus of Nazareth as the “Christ”, the Messiah. Their day is no longer the Sabbath day of yearning and hope. Their day is the “eighth day”, the day of Easter, Sunday, the day on which Christ rose from the dead and finally delivered and redeemed the world embroiled in sin and death. While the Jewish Christians initially kept the Sabbath, early on Gentile Christians celebrated the “Day of the Lord”, which followed the Sabbath, early on. Every Sunday should be a reflection of Easter, a continuation of Easter, as if the jubilation were too much for one day and radiates throughout all time.

Today, for many people, there is no longer any difference between a working day and Sunday. The huge machines still have to run. The service-based economy demands service on weekends. Shops

need shopping. Everyone hangs out whenever they can fit it in. Time has no structure anymore. There is no difference between celebration and everyday life. Celebration days are determined by the furniture store. Everything is possible at any time and smells of beer and a sausage sizzle. You'd think people would be happy with all this new flexibility. But they complain about the grey monotony of their days.
Can we reinvent Sunday? I don't believe it will be the

Question 184: How does the liturgy shape/impact time?

> We cannot live without Sunday. Don't you know that the Christian exists for the Eucharist and the Eucharist for the Christian?

Answer given by the **Abitene Martyrs** (305), Aturninus specifically, during interrogation over the accusation that they had taken part in the banned Sunday assembly

unions that save it – it will be the people who return together to Sunday's cultic roots. Sunday is not sacred because it's humane to put away the hammer or keyboard after six working days and dethrone work. Sunday has its centre in God. And it needs to be a feast – with everything that goes with it: the effort to make things beautiful, lots of time for each other, for love and for God, with flowers, festive songs, festive clothing, festive rituals, leisure time and breathing a sigh of relief in God's beautiful world.

Question 365: How do Christians make Sunday "the Lord's day"?

And perhaps the day of drama, revolt and tears will return when someone lays a finger/hand on the "sacred" Sunday, the feast of the redeemed.

What does "You must not bear false witness" mean?

This unit talks about
gossip, Donald Trump,
Alice in Wonderland,
a dishonest Nazi judge
and an incredibly brave young woman
and her friends
for whom the dissemination of the truth
was even more important than
their own lives.

4.47: How can you use social media in the right way?

It's quite possible that the American President also has a positive side. Yet one cannot currently think about the Eighth Commandment ("Thou shalt not bear false witness") without coming across Donald Trump, "alternative facts" and "truthful exaggeration".

Question 452: What does the Eighth Commandment require of us?

Question 456: What should you do if you have lied to, deceived or betrayed someone?

But it would be spreading "fake news" to say that he invented these two terms. It was his Government spokeswoman, Kellyanne Conway, who defended the President with the argument that Trump was talking about "alternative facts" when he was found to have lied. Nor is Trump the author of the "truthful exaggeration" that we find in Trump's bestselling "The Art of the Deal", described as "innocent hyperbole" and "a very effective form of marketing". In truth, Tony Schwartz, ghostwriter, wrote the book and has now ruefully confessed this in public, speculating that not only has Trump never written a book, he has also never read one from start to finish. The President, he said, is only interested in himself.

" A truth that's told with bad intent beats all the lies you can invent.

William Blake English poet (1757–1857)

There has long been a trend to deal with the truth "creatively". In Lewis Carroll's "Alice in Wonderland" there is the quaint philosopher Humpty Dumpty, who sums it up: "When I use a word, it means just what I choose it to mean – neither more nor less." Alice : "The question is, whether you can make words mean so many things." Humpty Dumpty smiles: "The question is – which is to be master? That's all." In classical philosophy one defined truth as *adaequatio intellectus et rei* – truth is the concordance of issue and reason. Everyone knows that is true. You have to tell it as it is. Otherwise you are lying. But humans are sinners, and even toddlers understand that you just have to scream loud and long enough to get attention and be rewarded. And thus, if the Eighth of the Ten Commandments does not intervene, an interest-based approach to the truth emerges.

Question 455: What does it mean to be truthful?

Nazi judge Freisler knew perfectly well that the students of the "White Rose" resistance group standing in front of him spoke the truth. He used "alternative facts" to get rid of them. They stood in the way of power. Power created its own truth. Twenty-two-year-old Sophie Scholl knew that she could save herself with a lie, but she told the raving Nazi henchman to his face, "Soon you will be standing where we are standing now." The same day, 22 February 1943, she was sentenced to death and beheaded with the guillotine. Sophie Scholl was a Christian; her favourite quote was a saying by the philosopher Jacques Maritain: "You need to have a tough mind and a tender heart." Indeed, you need that because the connection between truth and truthfulness is not negotiable from God's perspective. Trickery is not allowed. You have to bear witness to the truth, if necessary to the point of martyrdom. Nowhere is the story of the followers of Christ more refulgent than in the long line of martyrs who did not yield to power, and who rather gave their lives than serve a lie and betrayal.

Question 454: How strongly obligatory is the truth of the faith?

One could have imagined that the Second World War with its millions of dead would have meant a break in the culture of lying. But as early as 1949, author George Orwell had reason to write a prophetic book about lies and power: I'm talking about the novel "1984". It is as if Orwell already had an inkling then what political correctness would lead to. Orwell creates a totalitarian state in which words are forbidden or redefined; he calls it "Newspeak". The authority responsible for snooping on citizens becomes the "Ministry of Love"; concentration camps are called "pleasure camps"; the thinking

And you will know the truth and the truth will make you free

Jn 8:32

person becomes a "thought criminal". Are we so far removed from this fictional world? As far as the redefinition of words is concerned we have plenty of experience, since the child in the mother's womb was suddenly called "a cluster of cells", and unambiguous abortion a "termination". Newspeak is far from being unmasked. If I hear the phrase "women's rights" today, my ears tingle. What lies behind this beautiful phrase? Usually the lobby of pro-abortion advocates. "Hate crime" is also a flexible concept at the very least. Certain things that displease the nebulous community of right thinkers can no longer be said out loud in Facebook or you are "unfriended". The Eighth Commandment is as relevant today as it ever was: for courageous and upright people.

Question 453: What does our relationship with the truth have to do with God?

O God, how glorious: a single person or two who tell the truth can do more than many others put together! Through them the blind gradually discover the way again, and God gives them joy and courage.

St Teresa of Avila (1515–1582)

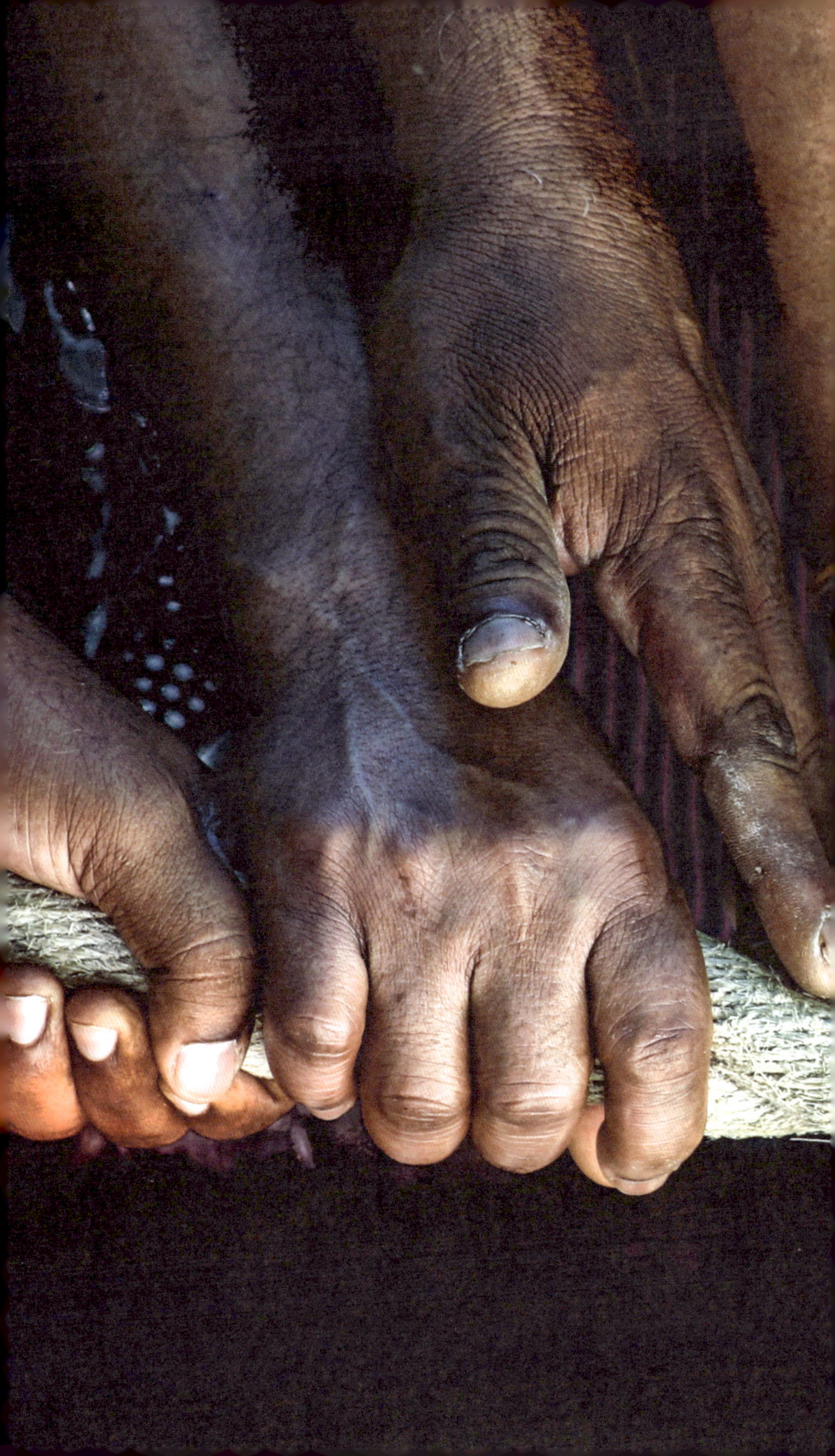

How do we act as socially responsible Christians?

This unit talks about
the fact that it is impossible
to regard Christianity as one's private concern.
One Christian is no Christian;
and someone who does not have
the happiness of everyone in mind
had better not refer to
the gospel.

An old-fashioned name for the Church is "mother". The famous theologian Henri de Lubac once said: "The Church is my mother because it gave me life. She is my mother because she keeps me alive and leads me ever deeper into this life."

SOCIAL TEACHING

Question 438: Why does the Catholic Church have her own social teaching?

Question 449: What significance do the poor have for Christians?

Question 427: Why is there no absolute right to private property?

The maternal aspect of the Church leads directly to her social teaching. For what is a good mother like? She is entirely concerned about her children. If the Church were only to disseminate clever teachings, if she were only to celebrate beautiful worship services, or only take care of the salvation of her children, she would be neither Church nor Mother. The Church must be interested in the holistic development of people: see that they have food and clean water, education, and work, that they can live in safety, that there is justice and that this mother's children do not tear themselves apart in quarrels.

The Church's history is not always glorious: the disciples slept when Jesus was afraid of death. Many Christians slept when witches were persecuted, when

slaves were put on ships, when Native Americans were expelled from their homeland, when Jews were taken from their homes, when the rainforest was deforested, when nuclear power plants were built, when abortion became a form of birth control. The Church's social teaching could have been written in many countries. But its beginnings lie in 19th century Europe, during the industrial revolution. Here too the Church woke up late. Children worked hard in the mines and workers died of hunger. Because Christians were asleep, Marxists took over their role.

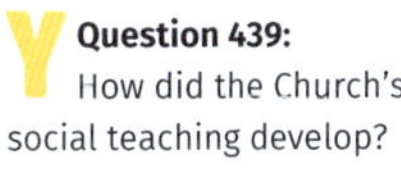

Question 439: How did the Church's social teaching develop?

It was only later that Christians reacted: they rediscovered the central social proposition in the Gospel of Matthew – this one revolutionary sentence from Matthew 25, with which Jesus identified himself with the social cause: "I was hungry and you gave me food, I was thirsty and you gave me something to drink, I was a stranger and you welcomed me, I was naked and you gave me clothing, I was sick and you took care of me, I was in prison and you visited me... Truly I tell you, just as you did it to one of the least of these who are members of my family, you did it to me."

Mt 25

Question 465: What attitude should a Christian take toward other people's property?

Question 89: To whom does Jesus promise "the kingdom of God"?

> If a Christian in these days looks away from the need of the poorest of the poor, then in reality he is not a Christian!
>
> **Pope Francis** in the Foreword to DOCAT

The Church's social doctrine developed from this tiny seed. Pope Leo XIII picked it up and, in his encyclical *Rerum Novarum*, wrote a harsh sentence that was completely unusual for a papal document at the time: "To defraud any one of wages that are [the worker's] due is a great crime."

Question 444: What does the Church's social doctrine say about the topics of labour and unemployment?

The principles:

HUMAN DIGNITY
SOLIDARITY
SUBSIDIARITY
COMMON GOOD

But what is this social doctrine at its core? It consists of four principles: the principle of the DIGNITY OF THE HUMAN PERSON, the principle of SOLIDARITY, the principle of SUBSIDIARITY and the principle of the COMMON GOOD. What do these mean?

Question 323: How can individuals be integrated into society in such a way that they nevertheless can develop freely?

The principle of the **dignity of the human person** means: "This teaching rests on one basic principle: individual human beings are the foundation, the cause and the end of every social institution" (*Mater et Magistra* 219). The individual human being in his or her dignity and freedom is under God's protection and thus supreme; the individual may never be "used" as cannon fodder or for whatever other purpose.

The **principle of solidarity** means that everyone must work together. This is the only way to create a just social order that guarantees everyone the fulfilment of their basic needs. Where individuals have no strength of their own to fulfil their elementary basic needs, society must help out.

The **principle of subsidiarity** means that tasks that can be taken on by smaller units are left to them to do. The task of the family is the education of their children; State bodies may intervene only in a subsidiary (= helping) way, if the family is overburdened.

The **principle of the common good** states that the authority of the State must be geared to the common good of everyone, especially the weakest, so that society does not become the playground for factional or individual interests.

In addition to these four principles, social teaching also deals intensively with issues like justice, peace and sustainable ecological development.

> By intervening directly and depriving society of its responsibility, the Social Assistance State leads to a loss of human energies and an inordinate increase of public agencies, which are dominated more by bureaucratic ways of thinking than by concern for serving their clients, and which are accompanied by an enormous increase in spending.
>
> **Pope John Paul II** (1920–2005) in *Centesimus Annus*, 48.

Someone once said that the Church's social teaching is one of its great untapped treasures. Because it is universal and cannot be appropriated by any power, nation, group or corporation, it has enormous power. Possibly the power to change the world.

Question 328: What can the individual contribute to the common good?

Prayer – what is that?

This unit talks about
whether our cries,
our words, our hymns
reach upstairs. Whether He hears us
or whether we are merely
wasting our words,
and our weeping and rejoicing
echo emptily in a
universe that is
deaf.

Question 470: What prompts a person to pray?

Question 468: What should a person yearn for most?

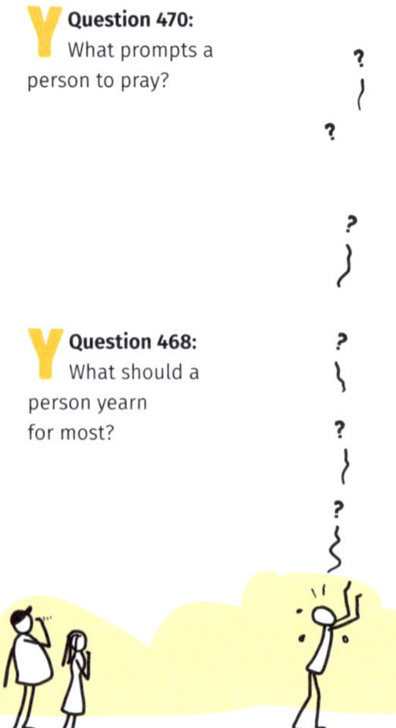

Praying is a part of Christianity. You can hear that said again and again. I remember when I was about 20 years old. Somehow I tried to be a Christian, but I cannot say that I really prayed. One day I found myself in a pew. I knelt there, so I was adopting a certain posture. But it was as if I was standing next to myself, watching myself. I did not leave my head. I just could not get beyond myself. Fortunately, later on, I was able to have the wonderful experience of being able to touch another reality – or rather, of being touched by it. Let's call this greater horizon of reality the presence of God.

I had a particularly deep experience of prayer in Taizé. If you haven't heard of the village of Taizé in French Burgundy you need to know that there is a community of hospitable monks there who take in thousands of young people year after year during the summer months. They come from all over Europe, often even from Africa, America and Asia. They come because in Taizé the reality of God is palpable, so to speak. And this is already the first experience one has of Taizé: that there are others who are similarly driven by a longing for God, just like myself. Okay – so I am not alone in the world with the innermost desire of my heart. The great Augustine (354-430) was right, then, when he said: "Great are You, O Lord, and greatly to be praised; great is Your power, and of Your wisdom there is no end. And man, being a part of Your creation, desires to praise You ... You have made us for Yourself, and our hearts are restless until they rest in You."

> In my opinion, prayer is nothing more than a conversation with a friend, whom we often like to meet alone to talk to because he loves us.

St Teresa of Avila (1515–1582)

Nothing's perfect in Taizé. You sleep in tents or in simple barracks. The bells ring three times a day. People stream in from all sides.
The church itself is a large "tent" which can be enlarged or reduced as needed. Before entering this church, one is confronted with teenaged helpers who carry signs before them. In different languages you can read a single word: Silence, *Stilte, Stille, Silenzio, Silencio*. This is the first basic rule of prayer: without silence nothing works. We must turn off all sources of noise, we must become calm inwardly and have some time so that something can happen in this silence.
So you enter this strange church in Taizé, in which there are no benches, only carpeting, and you are spellbound in an atmosphere of light and quiet. You

Question 469: What is prayer?

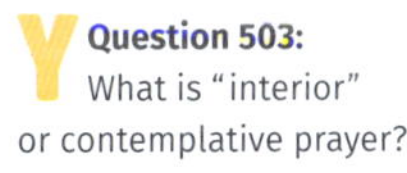

Question 503: What is "interior" or contemplative prayer?

3.7: How can I make time for prayer? Where is God in daily life?

❞ To pray does not mean to listen to oneself speaking. Prayer involves becoming silent, and remaining silent, and waiting until God is heard.

Søren Kierkegaard (1813–1855)

sit down on the floor and watch how the monks come as well and settle down in the middle of the room in silence and waiting for God. At some point, somebody starts a simple chant: *Veni, Sancte Spiritus* ... Come, Holy Spirit. It is repeated seemingly endlessly. Deeper and deeper, this call to prayer penetrates the soul. Then silence again. Then the Word of God that falls like a precious drop onto the mirror-smooth surface of my soul, and circles radiate out from there. Silence again. The felt presence of God. I left the church and could have cheered: wow, I had really prayed.

It works – and you don't even have to do much. God is here. And makes it happen ...

But Taizé gave me even more. We sat together in a group; we had never met before and had to agree on a common language first. We read the Holy Scripture together, we talked about it, gave each other insights. And then we prayed. Freely, just as our hearts suggested to us. Again, this "wow" feeling was there. It felt like in the early Church with the first Christians: "Now the whole group of those who believed were of one heart and soul" (Acts 4:32).

Y **Question 482:** What role did prayer play among the first Christians?

 **Acts 4:32**

" To pray means to think lovingly about Jesus. Prayer is the soul's attention that is concentrated on Jesus. The more you love Jesus, the better you pray.

Charles de Foucauld (1858–1916)

Today I can no longer imagine a life without prayer. Again and again I go to the Scriptures for inspiration, or I reread a few words that I have noted because they get me back on track. The first of these words is from St Therese of Lisieux: "For me, prayer is a surge of the heart; it is a simple look turned toward heaven, it is a cry of recognition and of love, embracing both trial and joy." That gets me back on track whenever I'm in a slump and I'm depressed. Lift up your heart! Just look up!

Y **Question 491:** Can you learn to pray from the Bible?

Y **Question 497:** Why does it help to use the saints as guidance when we pray?

How can we learn to pray?

This unit talks about
the reassuring message
that other than some crazy expectation
you don't need anything to get through to God.
What he wants is trust, closeness,
love, relationship.

How do you learn to tango? By learning tango steps with an experienced tango dancer. How do you learn to drive a car? By learning to drive with a good driving instructor and secretly practising in the parking lot. How do you learn to pray? Some people talk about having taught themselves. After all, there is the famous proverb "Need teaches one to pray." Someone who spent nights in air-raid shelters during the Second World War once assured me: "Believe me, there wasn't a single person there who did not pray!" But obviously the lesson did not stick for long. After the war came the economic miracle – and many who had escaped with their life quickly seemed to have forgotten that they had gone down on their knees before almighty God praying for salvation in the most dire of all needs. It might just have been "coincidence," they said to themselves, that bombs only hit the neighbour's house.

Y Question 486: Why should we petition God?

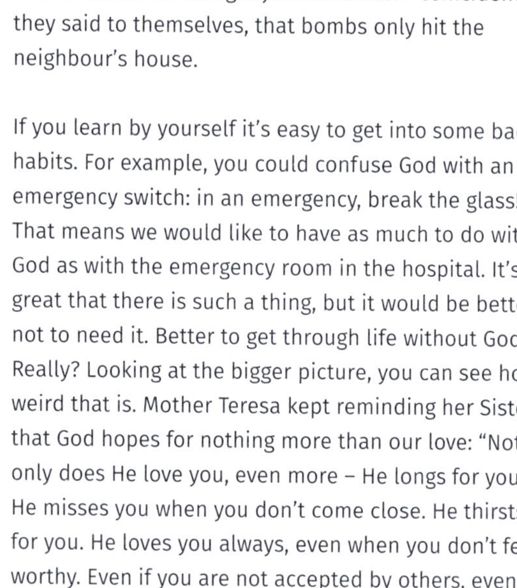

If you learn by yourself it's easy to get into some bad habits. For example, you could confuse God with an emergency switch: in an emergency, break the glass! That means we would like to have as much to do with God as with the emergency room in the hospital. It's great that there is such a thing, but it would be better not to need it. Better to get through life without God. Really? Looking at the bigger picture, you can see how weird that is. Mother Teresa kept reminding her Sisters that God hopes for nothing more than our love: "Not only does He love you, even more – He longs for you. He misses you when you don't come close. He thirsts for you. He loves you always, even when you don't feel worthy. Even if you are not accepted by others, even by yourself sometimes – He is the one who always accepts you."

What God wants – and why he has made prayer – is a relationship. A relationship of friendship. That you get in touch. That you are there for each other. That you can have an intimate exchange with each other. That you can rely on each other (as far as you can rely on human beings). To be in prayer is to be in relationship. In a steady relationship with God. Being a Christian is like being on Facebook where you can create your profile and also specify your relationship status. Many people write both on Facebook and regarding their relationship with God: "It's complicated." Yes, it really is complicated, even impossible if one wants to be a Christian but only phones in a few rituals. How can a relationship be kept alive if you don't have time to cultivate the relationship – that is, to pray?

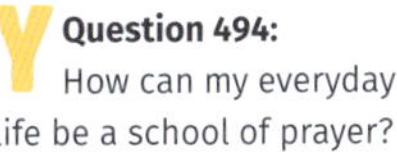

Question 494: How can my everyday life be a school of prayer?

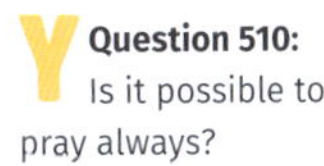

Question 510: Is it possible to pray always?

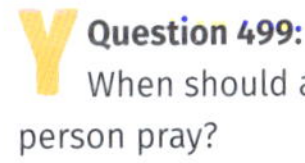

Question 499: When should a person pray?

> It is more important that we should remember God than that we should breathe
>
> **Gregory of Nazianzus** (ca. 329–390)

In YOUCAT's answer to Question 499 it says, "Someone who does not pray regularly will soon no longer pray at all." In the Scriptures, Paul even recommends: "pray without ceasing" (1 Thess 5:17). Of course, this does not mean that we are now to go on calling out to God from morning till night. We can truly cry out to God in our need, but there is one kind of prayer that is even more fundamental: "Give thanks in all circumstances; for this is the will of God in Christ Jesus for you" (1 Thess 5:18).

1 Thess 5:17–18

More important, then, than bombarding God with petitions (in mortal danger, for class assignments, or if you have screwed things up at work again) is obviously to get into an ongoing attitude of gratitude, and not deviate from this, not even for a moment. You can also learn by yourself, by walking through the world with open eyes and making it a habit to express

Question 488: Why should we thank God?

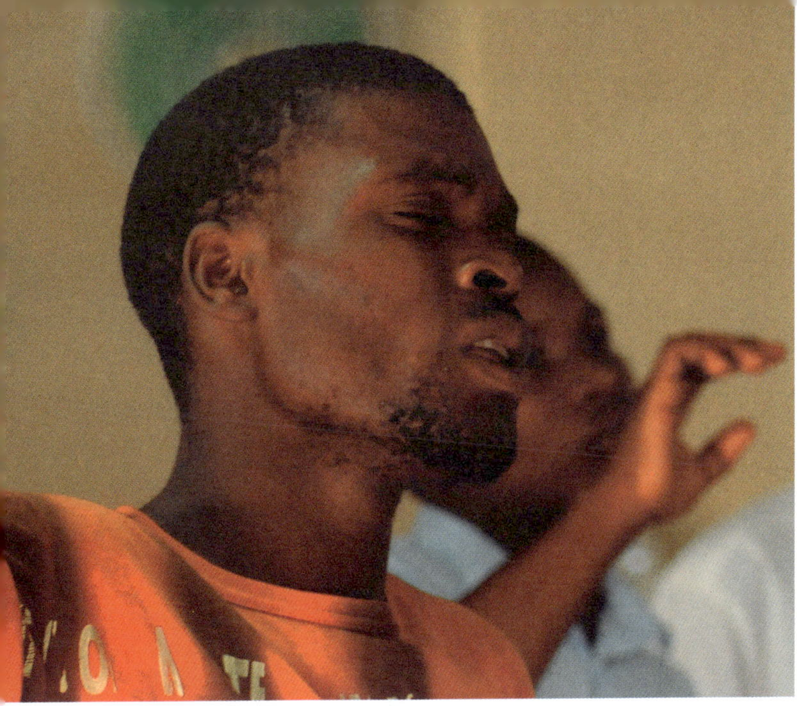

your amazement at the wonders of nature to its creator. As Psalm 8 puts it:

Question 473: How are the Psalms important for our prayer?

O Lord, our Sovereign,
  how majestic is your name in all the earth!...

When I look at your heavens, the work of your fingers,
  the moon and the stars that you have established;
what are human beings that you are mindful of them,
  mortals that you care for them?

 **Psalm 8**

Yet you have made them a little lower than God,
  and crowned them with glory and honour.
You have given them dominion over the works of your hands;
  you have put all things under their feet,
all sheep and oxen,
  and also the beasts of the field,
the birds of the air, and the fish of the sea,
  whatever passes along the paths of the seas.

3.8: How can I pray with a text from the Bible?

O Lord, our Sovereign,
  how majestic is your name in all the earth!

What is adoration?

This unit talks about
the fact that people shouldn't kneel before
anything or anyone except the living God.
Once you have found him,
you should not only
get down on your knees
in your thoughts,
but with your body
as well.

> Man, so long as he remains free, has no more constant and agonising anxiety than to find as quickly as possible someone to worship.

Fyodor M. Dostoyevski (1821–1881)

Question 293: Why did God give us "passions"?

Question 299: What is meant by a "virtue"?

What do Mother Teresa and Miley Cyrus have in common? Most people will say: not much. Miley undoubtedly looks better. Yet Mother Teresa has done more for the poor. But what do they have in common? They are both passionate. And they both have a thing about adoration. Mother Teresa advocated adoration wherever she went: "If you really want to grow in love ... come back to adoration." Miley also has songs on the subject, like the song "I adore you". Adoration is indeed a passionate word. It has something of absolute, crazy submission about it. Well, Miley has to maintain her wild image; she needs to be provocative. For example, she smoked what appeared to be a joint on stage.

And she came out with this song: "*When you say you love me / Know I love you more / And when you say you need me / Know I need you more / Boy, I adore you / I adore you.*" Is she serious? Anyone who submits to another person may seemingly prove how massive their love is. At the same time they make themselves small: "You can do whatever you want with me!" The worshipper gives up their dignity and will. In practical terms they have to expect/anticipate that one day they will get the boot from the object of their worship and be kicked away like a piece of dirt. American show business delivers trash of this kind every day: three months of adoration, then a break-up via WhatsApp, tears, drama, the end of the world, new eternal love, and so on. With Mother Teresa and her Sisters you can be sure that her adoration was not and is not about an Adonis with a sixpack. When Mother Teresa said, "I adore you," she always meant God.

But are we allowed to submit absolutely? Are we allowed to abase ourselves to this extent? Is it humanly allowable to make oneself so small and the other so big? Should we prostrate ourselves before someone, even if this "someone" is God? The answer is that we should not bow down before anything or anybody in the world; there is nothing in the world worth worshipping. We must submit only to the true God. To submit to anything that is not God through an act of adoration is why we have the word "idolatry". And now here's the twist: when we recognise the true God, we must not only submit – we want to submit. Then it's true: God is everything. We are nothing. "What do you have that you did not receive?" asks Paul in 1 Cor 4:7.

> To pray is not to recite prayers learned by heart, but to simply worship with or without words; to persevere at the feet of God in our will, with the intention of worshipping Him.
>
> **Bl. Charles de Foucauld** (1858–1916)

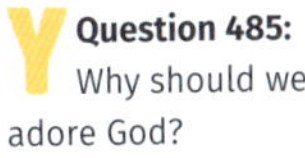

Question 485: Why should we adore God?

1 Cor 4:7

Question 355: "You shall not have strange gods before you." What does that mean?

A well-known priest once said, "All we have from ourselves is our sin." Otherwise we have everything from God. It is the fundamental act of the Christian faith to submit to the true God. Adoration is thus the prayer before all prayers. But this prayer presupposes that one does not fall into the hands of a pseudo-god.

> Where God is made great, men and women are not made small: there too men and women become great and the world is filled with light.

Pope Benedict XVI 11.09.06

Question 493: What are the characteristics of Christian prayer?

Question 496: Why do we need the Holy Spirit when we pray?

Phil 2:6-8

So how did Mother Teresa know that she was promoting worship of the true God? There really are religions in the world whose god I would not want to have inherited. A god who is not good to everyone but who prefers certain people and dislikes others – that is at best a caricature of God, not for a moment worth looking at. Mother Teresa knelt before a God who became unimaginably human in Jesus Christ: "who, though he was in the form of God, did not regard equality with God as something to be exploited, but emptied himself, taking the form of a slave, being born in human likeness. And being found in human form, he humbled himself and became obedient to the point of death — even death on a cross" (Phil 2:6-8). Not a dominant world ruler, but a humble, infinitely lovable world servant!

Jn 6:35

And then she discovered this little piece of bread in the monstrance: the body of Christ, here today, can be eaten today, is visible today, God's presence in close proximity. "I am the bread of life. Whoever comes to me will never be hungry, and whoever believes in me will never be thirsty" (Jn 6:35). Mother Teresa was filled with jubilation: "He is truly there in person, waiting for you."

“How great is the value of conversation with Christ in the Blessed Sacrament, for there is nothing more consoling on earth, nothing more efficacious for advancing along the road of holiness!”

Pope Paul VI, *Mysterium Fidei*

Henceforth she spent her “spare time” preferably before God. And she felt that the divine presence radiated outwards, that one really received something through adoration. “We find that through our daily Holy Hour our love for Jesus becomes more intimate, our love for each other more understanding, and our love for the poor more compassionate. Our adoration has doubled the number of our vocations ... The time that we spend in our daily conversation with God is the most precious part of the whole day.”

Y **Question 218:** What is the right way to honour the Lord present in the bread and wine?

3.14: What do I do during adoration?

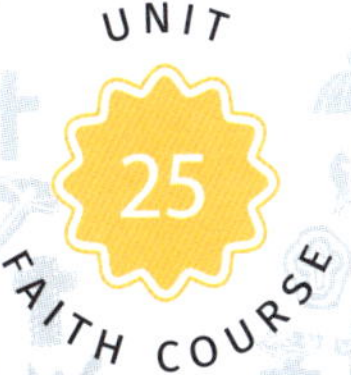

How does Jesus teach us to pray?

This unit talks about
how our human prayer
needs to go to Jesus' school.
To pray the Lord's prayer
means to walk in Jesus' words
as if we walked
an infallible path in his shoes
to the heart of all things.

Question 473: How are the Psalms important for our prayer?

Abba! Father!

One must learn to pray; Jesus's disciples already knew that. In Judaism, there was always prayer, even very intense and beautiful prayer. The Psalms alone prove this – powerful texts that are still prayed by millions of people all over the world, day after day. But the schooling the disciples received in their childhood, at the synagogue, at home, or with a rabbi was not enough for them. For them, Jesus was the specialist for all things God and the number one with regards to prayer. They saw not only how he kept withdrawing into solitude to pray, they also felt that he was permanently "in relationship" and that his inner life was always in a kind of radio contact. Sometimes, according to the evangelists, the disciples pulled Jesus out of prayer. Perhaps on such occasions they witnessed fragments of dialogue, such as the evangelist Luke tells us about on the Mount of Olives: "Father, if you are willing, remove this cup from me; yet, not my will but yours be done" (Luke 22:42).

Question 475: How did Jesus pray?

Question 476: How did Jesus pray as he was facing his death?

Lk 22:42

> God never ceases to be the Father of his children **St Anthony of Padua** (1193–1231)

In moments like these, the disciples had to perceive how intense Jesus' relationship with his Father was. Their Lord and Master was almost wrestling with his God: "In his anguish he prayed more earnestly, and his sweat became like great drops of blood falling down on the ground" (Lk 22:43).

Question 477: What does it mean to learn from Jesus how to pray?

Lk 22:43

And so, after he had "finished praying", the disciples approached him and said: "Lord, teach us to pray, as John taught his disciples" (Lk11:1).

Lk 11:1

What tricks and tips did Jesus have up his sleeve? How did it work? How often a day? Should you perhaps go out into the desert, throw yourself onto the ground? Raise your hands to heaven? Or what? Jesus didn't answer any of those questions. At any rate, the Bible does not tell us anything about this. Instead, he gave the disciples (and thus us too) a model prayer. We all know it: the Lord's Prayer. We can be sure: praying the Lord's Prayer means walking in the words of Jesus, as if we were walking on an infallible path, in his shoes, into the heart of all things.

Question 474: How did Jesus learn to pray?

Abba! Father!

For where does the Lord's Prayer lead us? The first word already says it: to our Father. We no longer think any more of it, but for Jewish ears it was different. God was considered the holy, the unapproachable, the unutterable. Jesus makes it clear: this sublime God is generally approachable with a primal human word, with the word Father. The fact that Jesus called God "Father" was undoubtedly noticed by the disciples. After all, their Lord had a unique son-father relationship with God.

Question 514: What position does the Our Father hold among prayers?

Question 515: Where do we get the confidence to call God "Father"?

But now Jesus was encouraging everyone to call him Father. He democratised his form of address to God. That was unheard of. Jesus was bringing the person praying (or "those who prayed") closer to God than ever before. To imagine that "the one up there" was like the merciful father in the parable of the prodigal son (Luke 15:11-32) – that was a downright religious upheaval! The Lord's Prayer revolutionised humankind's relationship with God. The once so distant God is now someone you may address intimately. God is the one you can come back home to after all the catastrophes and crises of your life – and you will find open arms. The fattened calf will be slaughtered. A feast is on the horizon.

> Teach me to serve you as you deserve;
> To give and not to count the cost;
> To fight and not to heed the wounds;
> To toil, and not to seek for rest;
> To labour, and not to ask for reward –
> except to know that I am doing your will

St Ignatius of Loyola (1491–1556)

1 Sam 3:9

After the salutation "Father", there is a second focus that permeates the Lord's Prayer: "Your will be done." Jesus refers to the formative experience of the people of Israel: that God speaks, that he calls, and that everything depends on the fact that one recognises this calling and responds to it with boundless trust. As Abraham did, as Isaac did, as Jacob did, as did the prophets: "Speak, Lord, for your servant is listening" (1 Sam 3:9). It is still today one of the people of Israel's most important prayers, the formula "Hear, O Israel! The LORD is our God, the LORD alone" (Dt 6:4) What is his will? Praying the Our Father is a lifelong exercise in the art of letting go of our will and doing

God's will passionately. Charles de Foucauld, one of the greatest spiritual teachers of the 20th century, empathised deeply with the Lord's Prayer and continued praying it in this wonderful way: "Father, I abandon myself into your hands; do with me what you will. Whatever you may do, I thank you: I am ready for all, I accept all. Let only your will be done in me, and in all your creatures. I wish no more than this, O Lord. Into your hands I commend my soul; I offer it to you with all the love of my heart, for I love you, Lord, and so need to give myself, to surrender myself into your hands, without reserve, and with boundless confidence, for you are my Father."

Y **Question 521:** What does it mean to say "Thy will be done on earth as it is in heaven"?

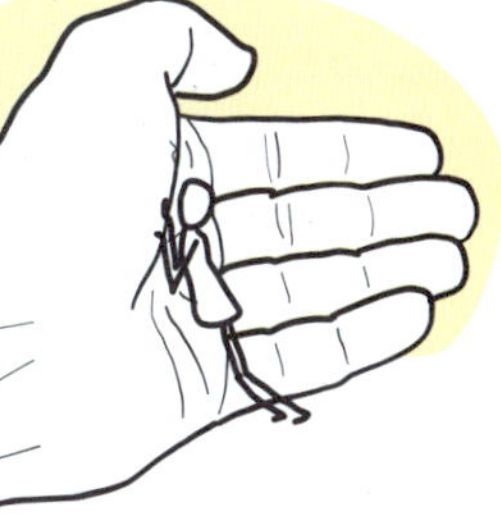

IHS
IHS
IHS

How do we say Yes to God?

This unit talks about
opting out of a
Christianity of empty words,
and entering into a Christianity of commitment.
It may cost you your career,
your friends, your reputation
but you will gain life.
A fleeting encounter with God
becomes a grand story.

Question 165: Why do we say "Amen" to the profession of our faith?

A lot of people get upset for being asked again and again at church to say "yes" to things they have never really thought about. Do you believe in God? Who can say that so precisely? ... Maybe, in good moments or when things are going really badly for me. Do you reject Satan? Whew! ... Are you ready to educate the children that God has given you in the faith? Of course you say "Yes", "Amen" so as not to be a spoilsport. Surely the priest won't question you too closely.

 Jn 6:35

 Jn 6:60

Jesus did things differently. Chapter 6 of John's Gospel is tough going. A carpenter and builder from Nazareth, who has not yet yet distinguished himself in any way, says: "I am the bread of life. Whoever comes to me will never be hungry, and whoever believes in me will never be thirsty" (Jn 6:35). Not only the Pharisees are outraged, but his friends, too, are at a loss. Was that really necessary: "This teaching is difficult; who can accept it?" (Jn 6:60).

Some leave, disillusioned. Jesus confronts the others who remain: "Do you also wish to go away?" This is the moment when Peter says: "Lord, to whom can we go? You have the words of eternal life" (Jn 6:68).

Jn 6:68

Some will have agreed wholeheartedly with what Peter said. They will have said "Amen". This word occurs 152 times in the New Testament alone. It is a statement of affirmation. Jesus uses it when he has something very important to say: "Amen, Amen, I say to you, whoever keeps my word will never see death!" (Or in some versions, Amen is replaced by "Very truly, I tell you"). When Jesus' audience says Amen, it means something like: Exactly! One hundred percent! Great! Entirely my opinion! Since the time of Jesus the "Amen" has been almost overused. Practically no prayer ends without everyone saying, "Amen!" How many times will that have been said with a half heart and an empty head? We have every reason to turn this empty word into an act of surrender again: Yes, Lord, I believe you. Amen! Yes, Lord, you have the words of eternal life. Amen.

Question 527: Why do we end the Our Father with "Amen"?

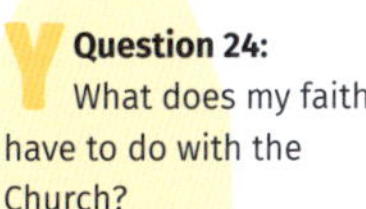

Question 24: What does my faith have to do with the Church?

That Jesus demands to be listened to, and obeyed, may be okay. But Catholic Christians not only listen to Jesus – they also listen to the Church, which makes Jesus accessible to them in word and sacrament. Jesus himself transferred his authority to the Church, which, in the Holy Spirit, should teach, proclaim and demand the Amen: "Whoever listens to you listens to me, and whoever rejects you rejects me, and whoever rejects me rejects the one who sent me" (Lk 10:16). There is a German hymn sometimes used for baptisms or confirmations that, if translated into English, would

Lk 10:16

read along the lines of: May my baptismal covenant always stand firm; I will listen to the Church. It might be less known today, but theologically it hits the mark. But then truth is concrete, specific, after all – and if a Catholic Christian today says: "I don't mind listening to Jesus but I couldn't care less about the Church", this person is also not taking Jesus seriously.

4.17: How does one become a saint?

Admittedly, the Church lives less from hard obedience and more from a much more intimate assent to God, like the assent of one particular young woman. In former times people said with murmuring admiration: "She spoke her Fiat." People then didn't have to worry that someone might be thinking of a brand of Italian car. They all knew the story of the maybe 15- or 16-year-old girl from Nazareth, who was visited by an angel sent from heaven who delivered an entirely outrageous proposal. The young woman was to be the mother of a divine child without help from any man. We are talking about Mary and the fact of faith that God could only come into the world because of this Amen, this assent, this okay that Mary gave. "Fiat" is Latin and means: "It shall be thus." The Amen transforms a vague "to be held as true" into a commitment, a commitment which responds to Jesus' commitment, who himself said "Yes" to his journey to the cross.

Question 84: Was Mary only an instrument of God?

The martyrs of the early Church died for their faith in that God who was revealed in Jesus Christ, and for this very reason they also died for freedom of conscience and the freedom to profess one's own faith - a profession that no State can impose but which, instead, can only be claimed with God's grace in freedom of conscience.

Pope Benedict XVI

> Live as though you were going to have to die as a martyr tomorrow

Bl. Charles de Foucauld (1858–1916)

Mary is, so to speak, the role model of faith. She provides space for God in herself, brings God into the world. In her own flesh, God becomes flesh (assumes concrete form, becomes human) from God, the true God from the true God. And she testifies to this, singing: "The Almighty has done great things for me." Mary is the first witness of Jesus. From then on she is a Christian who is a witness of Jesus. The Greek word for testament is *Martyria*. So the witness is the "martyr". Someone who goes to their death, if necessary, for Jesus and the truth of the Gospel.

Question 82: Isn't it improper to call Mary the "Mother of God"?

In February 2015, IS (Islamic State) published a propaganda video. IS henchmen had taken a group of Christians to a beach in Libya to slit their throats in front of rolling cameras. The aim of the video was to spread "a message written in blood to the nation of the cross." On the video one clearly hears two words: "Jarap Jesoa" – Lord Jesus!

Question 454: How strongly obligatory is the truth of the faith?

From Faith Course to Study Guide

Here you have

come to know essential **topics of the faith**. Again and again you were invited to visit catechism questions in **YOUCAT** to better understand the faith of the Catholic Church. Now, you may have a group or a circle of friends and want to do something together to bring new joy to your faith. Why not invite them to a regular **discussion of faith**?

Is that complicated?

No, it's very simple! Here's what to do. The **YOUCAT Study Guide** was developed for this very purpose and can be downloaded free of charge. The **YOUCAT Study Guide** has 26 parts like the Faith Course: For each faith course topic there is a matching Study Guide. The Study Guide always has the same structure.

Five elements

- Prayer
- Bible
- YOUCAT question
- Questions for discussion
- A challenging task

Five advantages

- No preparation necessary
- No further media required
- Tried and tested models for group work
- Room for your own ideas
- The ideal opening for a faith discussion

The faith course gives the leader of a group a framework for the conversation. But it also works the other way round: participants in the group can read it to deepen their understanding.

The ultimate goal:

To gain convictions that empower us in our identity as Catholic Christians and that make us confident in spreading the faith.

1

What do we know about God?

PRAY

Mein Herr und mein Gott!
Ich weiß so wenig von dir.
Manchmal denke ich, du bist himmelweit weg von mir.
Du musst schon zu mir kommen, in mein Herz und meinen Verstand, dass ich Vertrauen gewinne und eine Ahnung von dir bekomme.
Amen.

CONTEMPLATE

Einer liest die Bibelstelle laut vor.
Kurze Stille.

***Austausch**: Was hat euch besonders angesprochen?*

Röm 1, 20

Seit Erschaffung der Welt wird nämlich seine unsichtbare Wirklichkeit an den Werken der Schöpfung mit der Vernunft wahrgenommen, seine ewige Macht und Gottheit.

STUDY

1. YOUCAT Text Satz für Satz reihum lesen. Anschließend liest eine Person den Text am Stück vor.
2. Drei Minuten Stille.
3. Jeder liest ein Wort oder einen Satz laut vor, der ihm/ihr besonders aufgefallen ist – ohne Kommentar.
4. Erklärt in der nächsten Runde kurz, warum ihr den Satz ausgewählt habt (z.B. Erinnerungen, Fragen, ...).

Können wir die Existenz Gottes mit unserer Vernunft erkennen?

Ja. Die menschliche Vernunft kann Gott mit Sicherheit erkennen. [31–36, 44–47]

Die Welt kann ihren Ursprung und ihr Ziel nicht in sich selber haben. In allem, was es gibt, ist mehr, als man sieht. Die Ordnung, die Schönheit und die Entwicklung der Welt weisen über sich selbst hinaus und auf Gott hin. Jeder Mensch ist offen für das Wahre, das Gute und das Schöne. Er hört in sich die Stimme des Gewissens, die ihn zum Guten hindrängt und vor dem Bösen warnt. Wer dieser Spur vernünftig nachgeht, findet Gott.

DISCUSS

Diskutiert auch eigene Fragen zu diesem Thema!

***Treasure Book**: Nimm dir fünf Minuten Zeit und schreibe auf, was du nicht mehr vergessen willst.*

1. Hast du schon einmal gespürt, dass es Gott gibt?
2. Woran erkennt man, ob ein Mensch offen ist für das Wahre, Gute und Schöne?
3. Inwiefern kannst du Gott auch mit deiner Vernunft erkennen?
4. Würdest du dem Satz „Von nichts kommt nichts" zustimmen?

CHALLENGE

*Unsere **CHALLENGES** sind nur Vorschläge, die ihr zusätzlich zu euren Studyguidetreffen machen könnt. Ihr könnt sie auch durch stärkere, passendere, originellere oder bessere ersetzen. Teilt sie uns einfach mit an **feedback@youcat.org**.*

***#YOUCATChallenge**: Teilt eure Erfahrung auf Facebook oder Instagram.*

Frage eine Person in deinem Umkreis, wie sie Gott in ihrem Leben erkannt hat, und teile, was du gehört hast, beim nächsten Treffen mit deiner Studygroup.

Nimmst du diese Challenge an?

YOUCAT Studyguide

www.youcat.org

Index of names

Subject index

List of all questions from YOUCAT

Sacraments

Christian social teaching

List of all Biblical passages

Photo credits

Benedikt XVI./kathpedia S. 20; Maria Boeselager/Kommende junger Malteser S. 93; Jeremy Bishop in unsplash.com S. 66; Caecilia Engels S. 10; flickr.com S. 95; Lachlan Hardy/flickr.com S. 131; Heinrich Hoffmann Getsemane/pinterest S. 158; Jeronimo Lauricio/YOUCAT Brasil S. 20; Alexander von Lengerke S. 26, 84; Peter von Lengerke S. 118; L'Osservatore Romano S. 72; Oreste Schaller/ Libanon on Stage S. 106; Lukas Schlichtebrede S. 100; Nightfever Deutschland (www.nightfever.org) S. 152; http://questionsessentiellescolombes.overblog.com/2015/11/raisons-de-venir-a-persecutes-pour-sa-foi-partir-ou-mourir.html S. 169; Thomas Obermeier in Kunstsammlungen der Diözese Würzburg, 2019 86; Pixabay 13, 24, 40, 104, 115, 116, 122, 134, 139, 144, 150–151; pexels.com 16, 19, 22, 62, 101, 113, 133, 163; picture alliance/akg-images S. 65; Platytera, Griechisch-Orthodoxe Kirche (Alte Schule 3, 51645 Gummersbach, Deutschland, Ikonenmaler: Konstantinos Chondroudis) S. 54; Sven-Sebastian Sajak, Wikimedia Commons, Creative Commons-Lizenz by-sa.4.0 S. 118; Luc Serafin S. 19, 50, 52, 55, 59, 89, 164; Virginia State Parks/flickr.com S. 98; Wikimedia Commons (lizenzfrei) 12, 13, 15, 18, 21, 27, 30, 31, 34, 37, 38, 42, 45, 46, 48, 56, 57, 60, 63, 68,71, 75, 77, 80, 82–83, 87, 90, 103, 110, 117, 121, 128, 132, 143, 154, 160, 165, 168; Constanze Wilz S. 94; Katharina Wollkopf S. 108; Worship1/maxpixel.de S. 148; YOUCAT Foundation S. 32

The YOUCAT App

YOUCAT daily is an ideal companion for anyone who wants to grow in faith, **daily ...**

- ... the Gospel of the day on your smartphone
- ... a marching question from YOUCAT or DOCAT
- ... an inspiration from the international community or from saints and famous Christians

Five minutes a day. And in three years you can learn all about the faith of the Catholic Church.

On the Internet: **www.youcat.org/daily**

or:

Notes

Notes

Notes